MODERN AMERICAN HISTORY ★ A Garland Series

Edited by
FRANK FREIDEL
Harvard University

HOOVER'S DOMINICAN DIPLOMACY AND THE ORIGINS OF THE GOOD NEIGHBOR POLICY

E. R. Curry

Garland Publishing, Inc.
New York & London ★ 1979

Library of Congress Cataloging in Publication Data

Curry, Earl R 1933–
Hoover's Dominican diplomacy and the origins of the Good Neighbor Policy.

(Modern American history)
Bibliography: p.
Includes index.
1. United States—Foreign relations—Dominican Republic. 2. Dominican Republic—Foreign relations—United States. 3. United States—Foreign relations—Latin America. 4. Latin America—Foreign relations—United States. 5. Hoover, Herbert Clark, Pres. U.S., 1874–1964. I. Title. II. Series.
E183.8.D6C87 327.73'07293 78-62379
ISBN 0-8240-3629-8

All volumes in this series are printed on acid-free, 250-year-life paper.
Printed in the United States of America

CONTENTS

To Carolyn,

Kevin and

Amy

PREFACE

This book is about the twentieth century American practice of intervention in Latin America. By intervention I mean the threat or use of military occupation or actual supervision and control of the collection and disbursal of revenues to achieve a policy objective. To define intervention more broadly would necessitate the inclusion of economic and political pressures that all nations in a position to do so conventionally employ in their relations with each other. When confronted by such pressures, each nation weighs the advantages and disadvantages accruing from submission or resistance. In this sense, the foreign policies of most nations are meddlesome and interfering. It is obvious that when one nation possesses a preponderance of political and economic leverage, as is the case in relations between the United States and the other American republics, a forbidding quantity is added to the equation. In this circumstance, one is confined to assessing the wisdom of the policy objective and the farsightedness and good sense of the policy maker. In an imperfect world and especially in a world largely indifferent to its own imperfections, it adds little to our understanding of affairs to rail against the legitimacy of these conventional means.

Intervention, as defined above, and as exercised by the United States in the western hemisphere, was not a conventional means to a diplomatic end. It was the consequence of an assertion of virtual sovereignty in the Caribbean and Central America. Whether motivated by economic considerations or by perceived security requirements, the practice of intervention was disdainful of the claims of these states to independent and sovereign status when these got in the way of North American aims and interests. In this book it will be argued that intervention was retained as an alternative course of action in the Caribbean area until 1933. It will also be argued that the renunciation of the right to intervene was the minimal requirement to the reconstruction of United States relations with Latin American states on a basis that recognized equal status to the latter irrespective of the unequal distribution of power.

This study was first written as a Ph.D. dissertation in 1966. The present book is the result of extensive revision of that study after additional research in the Hoover and Stimson papers and the Stimson diaries. In truth, the hours spent pouring over the Hoover and Stimson papers were rewarded with a low yield. Where Latin American affairs are concerned, little was added to what was already known from published sources. The Stimson diaries were especially useful, however, as Stimson devoted a great deal of attention to relations with the Dominican Republic from the summer of 1930 to the summer of 1931. For a time, he seems to have hoped that the handling of Dominican affairs would provide a model for the approach to the rest of the Caribbean. But the Manchurian crisis and resórt to the moratorium as the device to provide temporary relief in the matter of international payments emerged as the chief concerns by the fall of 1931. Thereafter, Dominican affairs were given a low priority and received scant attention. It is my fair hope that, as a consequence of additional research and extensive rewriting, the thesis of the book is more sharply in focus than it was in the dissertation and that a more mature understanding of the secondary literature treating the origins of the Good Neighbor Policy has been acquired since graduate school days.

I wish to thank a number of individuals who in a variety of ways have had a hand in the making of this book: Frank Friedel, whom I have not had the pleasure of meeting, for reading the manuscript and recommending it, mutatis mutandis, for publication; William Cohen, my colleague at Hope College, for timely and helpful suggestions; Robert Wood of the Hoover Library in West Branch, Iowa and Judy Schiff, Chief of Archives and Research at Yale University, Sterling Library, for their courtesy and able assistance; Hope College for its financial assistance in the finishing stages of preparing the manuscript; and finally my wife Leslie, for candid criticism and proof-reading of the final draft, and for patience and tolerance. All errors and instances of awkwardness or lack of clarity are, of course, my own responsibility.

E.R. Curry

CHAPTER I

INTRODUCTION

At the risk of raising what John Higham has called "the menace of dead issues," the intent and purpose of the following study is to demonstrate that a Good Neighbor Policy for the western hemisphere did not emerge before 1933. There was no Good Neighbor Policy nor any Good Neighborliness, if Bryce Wood's distinction may be employed, until such time as the United States was prepared to commit itself to a course of non-intervention in the internal affairs of its hemispheric neighbors. No North American administration committed itself to such a policy from the time the subject became a matter of concern in the twentieth century until the advent of the New Deal. The conclusion of the study that follows is that if it can be said that a Good Neighbor policy once characterized relations between the United States and Latin America, then its origins no more than its successful implementation will be discovered before 1933.

During the 1930's, when the New Deal blazed with radical rhetoric and healed with pragmatism, few doubted that the Good Neighbor Policy was a Rooseveltian creature and a clear departure from the Latin American policies of previous twentieth century administrations. A "new deal" for Latin America was viewed as a natural corollary to Roosevelt's New Deal for the American people. On the other hand, before 1945, Herbert Hoover was associated in the public mind with the single interest politics of the 1920's that, after 1929, had created the long lines of jobless seeking work where none existed, with breadlines having at their end too little bread, with Hoovervilles and Hoovershirts. Just as his domestic policies were associated with the "Republican ascendancy" of the 1920's, so too was his hemispheric policy. Where Latin America was concerned, informed critics readily agreed that Hoover's intentions were good. It was further conceded that he genuinely wanted and actively sought friendlier relations between the United States and its hemispheric neighbors. Finally, however, he failed because his Latin American policy adhered too closely to the course set down by his twentieth century predecessors. The attitudes, habits of mind and practices of the United States during the Hoover presidency fell far short of the innovations introduced by Roosevelt after 1933.[1]

This interpretation underwent substantial revision after World War II. The reasons for it are to be found in the insecurities of the post-war world and the impact this condition had on the historian's enterprise. By the late 1940's, the glamour of the New Deal was fading and the bitterness of the depression years had receded from sharp memory. The nation was faced with the challenge of the Cold War. The threatening nature of these crises ridden years called for a setting aside of the class antagonisms aroused during the 1930's. Business, labor, farmers and ethnic minorities united against a common

---

[1]Sumner Welles. The Time for Decision. (New York and London, 1944) pp. 191-192.

foe. Partially in response to the national state of mind taking shape in this period, a school of historians matured that held that conflict between contending economic and social forces in the 1930's, as in earlier periods of American history, was more apparent than real. These historians maintained that Hoover, after all, could not be blamed for the depression, and his policies to counteract its effects, far from being ineffectual or lacking in compassion, were on the verge of realizing a sustained recovery when Roosevelt was elected. By the time of his death in 1964, his defenders were attributing to Hoover the inspiration for much of the New Deal program that came after 1933.

Just as Hoover came to be viewed favorably as an innovator in domestic policy, so too did he in the formulation of his Latin American policy. So much has his stock gone up, in fact, that the weight of recent scholarship credits Hoover with initiating the Good Neighbor Policy while conceding that Roosevelt expanded upon it and had greater success in implementing it. The leading proponent of this view is Alexander De Conde. In his 1951 work, Hoover's Latin American Policy, he contends that the Good Neighbor Policy originated with Hoover, even to the extent of using the name, and that Roosevelt inherited it and enlarged upon the fortune.[2] In support of his thesis, De Conde argues that Hoover's goodwill trip to eleven Latin American countries between his election and inauguration

---

[2]Alexander De Conde. Hoover's Latin American Policy. (Stanford and London, 1951) p. 124.

achieved its intended purpose. In addition, Hoover gave considerable attention to Latin American policy in several public addresses after his inauguration in which he attempted to undo or at least to explain away past offenses. The Hoover administration also adopted the pre-Wilson de facto recognition policy except in Central America where the matter was governed by a treaty negotiated between the United States and the five Central American republics. But De Conde rests his case, finally, on the release in 1930 of the Clark memorandum, a State Department study that denied that intervention by the United States in the internal affairs of its hemispheric neighbors was justified by the Monroe Doctrine. Then, as if to prove the significance of this document, it is pointed out that no new interventions were initiated by the Hoover administration.[3] Robert Ferrell seconds this interpretation in his broader treatment of Hoover's foreign policy, <u>Diplomacy During the Great Depression</u>.[4]

The accounts by De Conde and Ferrell deal wholly with Hoover's policies. But similar conclusions are reached by authors whose primary concern and sympathies are with Roosevelt's policies. Dexter Perkins, in his one volume survey of the history of the Monroe Doctrine, writes that the Good Neighbor

---

[3]<u>Ibid</u>. pp. 48-50.

[4]Robert H. Ferrell. <u>American Diplomacy in the Great Depression: Hoover-Stimson Foreign Policy, 1929-1933</u>. (New Haven, Conn. and London, 1957) pp. 215-233.

Policy was ". . . embarked upon by Mr. Hoover and Mr. Stimson and . . . brilliantly and effectively expanded and carried through by Mr. Roosevelt and Mr. Hull . . . ."[5] Similarly, in an absorbing and otherwise incisive work, The Western Hemisphere Idea, Arthur P. Whitaker maintains that ". . . the Good Neighbor Policy was born under Hoover, though it was baptized and came to maturity under Roosevelt."[6] In his survey of United States-Latin American relations, J. Lloyd Mecham is disdainful of attempts to discover the paternity of the Good Neighbor Policy. Yet, he is unable to resist the temptation to draft his own genealogical chart and finally credits Hoover with procreation and Roosevelt with adoption and the successful rearing of the Good Neighbor Policy to maturity.[7] Lloyd Gardner's enlightening study, Economic Aspects of New Deal Diplomacy, while chiefly concerned with discovering the economic motives behind the Good Neighbor Policy, nevertheless concludes that the policy was the culmination of the thinking of the decade preceding Franklin Roosevelt's inauguration. "By 1933," Gardner writes, ". . . the future course of inter-American relations had been pretty well set. The Good Neighbor Policy had been poured like hot liquid metal into this mold and then dumped out all shiny and new in Roose-

---

[5]Dexter Perkins. Hands Off: A History of the Monroe Doctrine. (Boston, 1941) p. 347.

[6]Arthur P. Whitaker. The Western Hemisphere Idea. (Ithaca, New York, 1954) p. 135.

[7]J. Lloyd Mecham. A Survey of United States-Latin American Relations. (Boston and New York, 1965) pp. 112-114.

velt's inaugural speech."[8]

Two other works, because of certain refinements that they impose upon this interpretation, warrant a fuller explanation than that given for the studies reviewed thus far. In the first of these, Are We Good Neighbors?, Donald Dozer refrains from making any categorical statement about the origins of the Good Neighbor Policy. It is plain, nevertheless, that Dozer believes that the policy began before 1933. He argues that during the 1920's American policy makers became concerned about deteriorating relations with the Latin American republics and determined that something other than the "big stick" was required to make repairs. The Hoover administration moved to reduce the bitterness of Latin American attitudes toward the United States by the "overt abandonment of intervention" and other acts of repentance and goodwill.[9] Hoover undid much of his own policy, Dozer qualifies, when he signed the Smoot-Hawley Tariff Act in 1930 and because he was slow in withdrawing the marines from Nicaragua and Haiti. While Dozer concedes much to the intentions of the Hoover administration, it is equally plain that he believes that Roosevelt more ably implemented the Good Neighbor Policy. He attributes Roosevelt's

---

[8]Lloyd C. Gardner. Economic Aspects of New Deal Diplomacy. (Madison, Wis., 1964) p. 51. [It should be noted that in his inaugural address, Roosevelt did not single out Latin America as the object of the policy of the good neighbor. The phrase was incorporated in a very general, even platitudinous, declaration and encompassed the world.]

[9]Donald Dozer. Are We Good Neighbors? Three Decades of Inter-American Relations, 1930-1960. (Gainsville, Fla., 1959) p. 12.

success to his freer trade policies and to the domestic reforms that he advanced. Latin Americans, Dozer points out, regarded the latter as a move away from the shabby materialism which they thought characteristic of North American culture.[10]

Finally, Bryce Wood, in an excellent study, The Making of the Good Neighbor Policy, goes further than anyone to credit the origins of the policy to the Roosevelt administration. He arrives at this conclusion, however, by drawing a distinction between the Good Neighbor Policy and the spirit of Good Neighborliness. The former, because it pertains to such matters as the reciprocal trade agreements, cooperation in the defense of the hemisphere and other actions immediately affecting relations between the United States and the Latin American countries, belongs to Roosevelt. The latter, Good Neighborliness, predates the New Deal. According to Wood, if those who have attributed to Hoover the origins of the Good Neighbor Policy spoke instead of Good Neighborliness, they should be on safer ground. The heart of Good Neighborliness, Wood contends, was a commitment to non-intervention in the internal and external affairs of the Latin American republics, and Hoover as well as Roosevelt gave primacy to non-intervention as "the highest policy objective."[11] He argues further that the importance placed on non-intervention grew out of the conviction emerging in the

---

[10]Ibid. pp. 14-24.

[11]Bryce Wood. The Making of the Good Neighbor Policy. (New York, 1961) p. 132.

1920's that there were equally effective but less crude ways to achieve American goals in this hemisphere, that military intervention was expensive and that there had been a dramatic shift in public opinion in the United States against the policy of intervention. He concludes that,

> In this sense three administrations each played a part in transforming the peaceful desires of the people of the United States into policies in which all have reason to claim some, if different, shares. There is satisfaction here for members of both political parties, and little reason for political argument....[12]

Though not exhaustive, this sketch of the literature on the question suffices to indicate the range and direction of the views taken by the best and most recent scholarship. It is fair to say that the conclusion reached by all of these accounts is that the Good Neighbor Policy, or Good Neighborliness, originated with the Hoover administration. Each of the authors, to a lesser or greater degree, credits Roosevelt with following through on the policy with more success than its progenitor. In this sense, the Good Neighbor Policy is viewed as the product of the accumulated wisdom of national leaders from, chiefly, two administrations.

It is discomforting to find oneself at odds with such an array of informed intelligence. Yet, each of the authorities cited has overlooked, misunderstood, or is in error respecting the one ingredient essential to the making of the Good

---

[12]*Ibid.* p. 135.

Neighbor Policy: a firm and publicly avowed renunciation of the right of intervention and a performance record that would indicate that the pledge was given in good faith. At no time during his tenure did Hoover ever commit his administration to a policy of non-intervention in Latin America. Without such a commitment, his other efforts to improve the hemispheric relations of the United States were destined to fall short of establishing a Good Neighbor Policy or Good Neighborliness. Until such time as the United States was prepared to commit itself to non-intervention, whatever advantages its trade policies may have afforded and however adept its public relations, no administration could have established credibility in Latin America. What the Latin American republics demanded was a decent regard for their independence and sovereignty irrespective of the disparities in the distribution of power. United States policies of intervention in the Caribbean were seen by Latin Americans as a denial of that independence and sovereignty. Roosevelt was prepared to commit the United States to non-intervention; Hoover was not. And therein lay the difference.

There are two ways of studying Hoover's Latin American policy to show that it lacked this essential ingredient, Dozer and Wood to the contrary notwithstanding. First, an examination of the general considerations that underlay the Hoover adminstration's policies in the hemisphere will reveal that they were not new. They were inherited from Charles Evans Hughes, Secretary of State to Harding and to Coolidge until 1925, and were shot through with the same reservations, qualifications and reluctance that had prevented his hemispheric policy from allaying Latin American suspicions of the northern collosus. If the Hoover administration's Latin American policy was such that it warrants credit for originating the Good Neighbor Policy, then advocates of that view would be on more defensible ground had they placed the credit with Hughes. Secondly, it will be demonstrated that the Hoover administration was not prepared to commit the United States to a policy of non-intervention in Latin America. Proof of this does not rest alone upon the failure to proclaim such a doctrine. A review of United States relations with the Dominican Republic from 1929 to 1933 will show that on three separate occasions the threat of intervention was held out as a possible if unwanted measure to discourage developments regarded as inimical to the interests of the United States or certain of its citizens.

A study of relations between the United States and the Dominican Republic is especially suited to the exploration of the origins of the Good Neighbor Policy. In no Latin American country more than here were economic supervision and military intervention more in evidence nor carried further toward their logical conclusions. The American naval officers who held all of the posts in the Dominican government from 1916 to 1924 sought recognition as the legitimate government in Santo Domingo. They received it from Nicaragua, another "client" state. All the problems that American policy makers would encounter in retreating from the twentieth century record of intervention can be discovered in the history of Dominican affairs after 1924. The whys and wherefores of the American supervision of Dominican finances that began in 1904 and the military occupation of the republic undertaken in 1916 are the subjects of the remainder of this chapter.

The history of the Dominican Republic in the nineteenth century is at least as unhappy as that of any nation in the hemisphere.[13] Its course to independence after 1808 was uneven and pursued only reluctantly. It was subject to recurring invasions from Haiti, victimized by the intrigues of French and Spanish diplomacy, exploited by unscrupulous lenders from England, the Netherlands and other European states and subjected to the mindless conspiracies of North American political entrepreneurs. When free of these plagues, this small garden was plowed, seeded and harvested to exhaustion by its own authoritarian and irresponsible political elite. Not infrequently, these forces combined or worked at odds to retard economic development and demoralize the country politically.

By the middle of the 1870's the threat of further invasions from Haiti had been removed and the intrigues of Spain and France had subsided. These developments brought no improvement to the conduct of Dominican government. A new generation of political leaders proved to be as corrupt and unresponsive

---

[13]Sumner Welles. Naboth's Vineyard: The Dominican Republic, 1844-1924. 2 Vols. (New York, 1928) [This is the best account of the history of the Dominican Republic and its relations with the United States and the European powers to 1924. Also useful is: Charles C. Tansill. The United States and Santo Domingo, 1798-1873. (Baltimore, 1938)]

to the popular will as had the old. In 1882, Ulises Heureaux inaugurated a brutal dictatorship that ended only with his assassination in 1899. Heureaux's regime was not only politically repressive but was flagrantly dishonest as well. The republic, nearly bankrupt when Heureaux had seized power, could not pay the extravagant costs of his dictatorship from its own meagre resources. To obtain funds, Heureaux followed the practice of his predecessors and borrowed heavily from foreign creditors pledging customs receipts as security. By 1903, the debt had reached an amount beyond the capacity of the Dominican government to pay.

Most of this debt was owed to European creditors but the United States became directly involved through the San Domingo Improvement Company, an American firm. During the 1890's, this company had bought up some of the bonds held by European creditors and claimed that its bond holdings amounted to $11,000,000. As security the Improvement Company had been granted mining and construction concessions. By 1903, the company had reached an impasse in its relations with the Dominican government and appealed to the United States government to act on its behalf.[14]

The United States would not intervene as the Improvement Company seemed to have hoped. It did enter into negotiations with the Dominican government, however, with the result that the company's claims were arbitrated. A settlement was reached

---

[14]Welles. Naboth's Vineyard. II. pp. 584-587.

placing the value of the company's claims at $4,500,000. Bonds for this amount were bought by a New York banking house and the Improvement Company was removed from its involvement in Dominican affairs. The new bonds were secured by the receipts from four Dominican customs-houses, the most important being at the northern port of Puerto Plata. The bonds were to be paid by monthly installments and at any time that the regular payment was not made the United States government had the right to take over the collections at these ports.[15]

The United States had taken a more active interest in Dominican affairs for another reason. Since the war with Spain, the United States had begun to assert itself as one of the great world powers. If this was an undefined feeling on the part of most Americans, it was articulated for them by a group of influential Republicans led by Theodore Roosevelt, Henry Cabot Lodge, Alfred T. Mahon and others. It was this attitude that had led to the construction of the Panama Canal and had made it imperative, by 1904, that the United States exercise the predominant influence in the Caribbean approaches to the Isthmus of Panama. None of the European powers could be permitted to extend their influence in this area thereby jeopardizing the security of the canal zone.

At the same time, however, it was recognized that the United States could not deny to these powers the right to redress their

---

[15]Melvin M. Knight. The Americans in Santo Domingo. (New York, 1928) pp. 20-21.

just grievances with the Caribbean republics unless it intended to do it for them. This was the problem facing the United States in the Dominican Republic. When, in October, 1904, the Dominicans failed to make the second installment on the Improvement Company award, the United States took possession of the customs-house at Puerto Plata. The French and Italian governments responded by threatening to seize control of the customs-house at Santo Domingo. At that point the Dominican government proposed that the United States take over collection of customs at all of the ports of the Republic. "This," one critic has written, "was not a free and spontaneous move, but a bid for common bondage as the alternative to dismemberment."[16]

Whether "free and spontaneous" or not, this same proposal had been made in 1903--before the Improvement Company settlement had been reached--by Carlos Morales, provisional president of the hour. His proposal had been supported by the Horacista Party--that is, the followers of Horacio Vásquez--the most popular and representative political group in the Republic. The Dominicans hoped that by removing the customs-house as a source of patronage and graft the revolutionary impulse would be quieted.[17]

The United States had not given serious consideration to the proposal at the time. In 1904, however, the presence of

---

[16]*Ibid*. p. 22.

[17]Welles. *Naboth's Vineyard*. II. pp. 612-613.

the threat of European intervention prompted President Roosevelt to accept the renewed offer. A convention was negotiated by which the United States would administer the collection of Dominican customs through an officer, the Receiver General of Dominican Customs, appointed by the President of the United States. According to the Convention, the United States would aid the Dominicans in negotiating an adjustment of its debt of $29,500,000. It further stipulated that collections from customs would be divided by 55-45 ratio, the larger amount to be retained by the General Receiver for payment of the debt and the smaller to be given to the Dominican government.[18]

The United States Senate failed to take any action on the treaty, however, because of objections to the feature involving the United States in the adjustment of the debt. Roosevelt, in 1905, put the agreement into effect, nevertheless, by means of a modus vivendi signed with the Dominican government. This instrument was to remain in effect until the Senate acted one way or the other. During the next two years the Dominican debt was adjusted downward to $17,000,000 and a loan for $20,000,000 was obtained from Kuhn, Loeb and Company with which to pay off the external debt and leave the Dominicans with a cash balance. With the objectionable feature removed the Senate approved the

---

[18] Ibid. pp. 624-630. [The outstanding debt of $29,500,000 included the internal debt amounting to $9,500,000, a nominal, or face, value. Later the estimate of the total amount of the external and internal debt was revised upward to a nominal value of $31,800,000.]

Convention in 1907.[19]

For an understanding of issues that were later to arise out of the Convention, a brief mention of its principal provisions at this point would be helpful. It provided for the appointment of a General Receiver in the manner described above. It provided that $100,000 per month would be set aside for the payment of interest and principal of the loan. Furthermore, one-half of all customs collections over $3,000,000 in any year would also be set aside for retirement of the debt. It was stipulated that the Dominican government could not increase its debt nor modify its tariff except by approval of the United States as long as any of the bonds were outstanding.

In the most recent and comprehensive study of this episode Dana G. Munro has observed that Roosevelt exaggerated the danger of European intervention when presenting the Convention to the Senate. This was not, however, a deliberate attempt to misrepresent the facts of the case, for the danger was real enough in Roosevelt's mind. "It seems clear," Munro wrote, "that he (Roosevelt) felt that the establishment of a customs receivership . . . was the only means by which European intervention could be avoided."[20]

---

[19] Ibid. pp. 623-628. [The external debt was reduced by negotiations with creditors from a nominal value of $21,000,000 to $12,500,000; the internal debt was reduced from the adjusted nominal value of approximately $4,500,000 to $2,800,000, making the total adjusted debt, including interest, $17,000,000. See Appendix I.]

[20] Dana G. Munro. Intervention and Dollar Diplomacy in the Caribbean, 1900-1921. (Princeton, New Jersey, 1964)

Moreover, Munro continued, the danger of intervention by one or more of the European powers was not non-existent. On the contrary, his contention is that the Europeans were in no mood to acquiesce in a situation in which American creditors were collecting their debts through control of customs-houses at Puerto Plata and three lesser ports while European creditors were denied the opportunity to collect their debts by the same device. Sumner Welles wrote in this same vein when he argued that it was no longer possible for the United States to deny to the European powers the right to redress their grievances--grievances which in that age were considered just--against certain of the Latin American countries that, counting on protection by the United States, flagrantly disregarded their obligations. "The continued interpretation of the Monroe Doctrine in that manner," Welles wrote, "would lead almost inevitably to war . . . with one or more of the European Powers."[21]

During the first six years that the receivership was in operation the Dominican Republic experienced a peace and quiet unknown since the halcyon days of the Spanish Empire. This was more the result of the administration of its president, Ramon Cáceres, than it was of the blessings of the receivership. It is true, nevertheless, that the receivership arrangement provided the Dominican government with more income than it had ever before realized from customs. It was Cáceres, however,

---

[21]Welles. Naboth's Vineyard. II. p. 619.

who provided the honest management of these funds. He was able as well as honest and, while he dealt quickly and firmly with would-be revolutionaries, his was a democratic administration.[22]

The political chaos that descended upon the Republic after the assassination of Cáceres in 1911 supports the argument that it had not been the receivership that had brought the stability of the preceding six years. Political anarchy led to financial instability that honest and efficient collection of customs could not prevent. As one provisional government followed another, money was borrowed--by forced loans when necessary--from Dominicans in order to buy off revolutionary leaders when that was possible and to suppress them when it was not. For their part the revolutionaries extracted money from those who had any in the areas they controlled, promising to repay when they gained control of the government.[23]

The reaction to these events by the Taft administration was predictable. Philander C. Knox, Taft's Secretary of State, has been characterized by Sumner Welles as brilliant and able, but in spite of these advantages, ". . . he remained a lawyer rather than a statesman . . ." whose foreign policy ". . . was determined by the immediate requirements of a limited privileged class . . . rather than by a true appreciation of the ultimate

---

[22]Ibid. Chap. XI. pp. 640-698. [Cáceres was a close political associate of Horacio Vásquez and was also the man who assassinated Ulises Heureaux.]

[23]Munro. Dollar Diplomacy. p. 266.

national interest."[24] Knox regarded the flotation of internal bonds by Dominicans as an increase in the public debt, and as such, a violation of the Convention of 1907. He had no patience at all with the political feuds between the several factions vying for control of the government. In his view the petty affairs of the Dominicans were interfering with the efficient conduct of the more important financial affairs of American businessmen. He intended to put an end to this foolishness.[25]

To achieve this end, Knox interfered with the attempts by Dominicans to settle their political crises and forced the resignation of a provisional government they had selected in 1912. He threatened intervention by the United States if his advice was not acceded to, an action ". . . plainly foreign to the treaty rights of the United States."[26] In 1913, he sent a commission to the Republic to mediate between the warring factions resulting in the selection of the Archbishop of Santo Domingo, Adolfo Nouel, as provisional president. Nouel was acceptable to all Dominicans concerned because he had no ties to any party. Neither, however, did he have any solid base of support or initial desire for the presidency. He was a well-intentioned but, through no fault of his own, ineffectual administrator.[27]

This was the situation facing Woodrow Wilson when he assumed

---

[24]Welles. Naboth's Vineyard. II. p. 698.

[25]Ibid. pp. 693-694.

[26]Ibid. p. 726.

[27]Ibid. p. 726.

office on March 4, 1913, and matters rapidly worsened thereafter. Nouel, disgusted with the venality of Dominican politicians and wholly unable to manage them, resigned on March 13, in spite of American pleas that he remain in office a while longer. A new provisional president was selected by the Dominicans but the situation degenerated into anarchy as local caudillos arose in open revolt against the government and each other.

The approach by Wilson to a settlement of these difficulties, and in fact, his approach to the entire field of foreign policy, proceeded from different assumptions than those held by his twentieth century predecessors. Where the basis of Roosevelt's policies had been primarily political expediency, and Taft's economic self-interest, Wilson's was morality and idealism. Of this basis of Wilsonian diplomacy, and that of his Secretary of State, William Jennings Bryan, Arthur S. Link has written that,

> . . . both . . . shared the assumptions and ideals that provided the dynamic for New Freedom diplomacy. Both were men of good will and noble intentions. Both were at heart moralists, who viewed international relations and America's role in World affairs in terms of immutable principles, not in terms of expediency.
>
> . . . both were fundamentally missionaries of democracy, driven by inner compulsions to give other people the blessings of democracy and inspired by the confidence that they knew better how to promote the peace and well-being of other countries than did the leaders of those countries themselves.[28]

---

28 Arthur S. Link. Wilson: The New Freedom. (Princeton, New Jersey, 1956) pp. 277-278.

The consequences of this attitude for Wilson's Latin American policy became apparent almost immediately after he assumed office when he came into conflict with the thoroughly disgusting dictatorship of Victoriano Huerta in Mexico. His early preoccupation with Mexican affairs influenced his policy generally in the Caribbean. He became convinced that what these countries needed was honest and democratic leadership and that it was the moral obligation of the United States to see that they received it.[29] When it came, intervention in the Dominican Republic was primarily a product of this view of the motives that should guide American policy. By assuming at the outset that the United States knew what leaders and what governmental forms were best for Latin Americans, it was possible to rationalize any action necessary to achieve the desired result.

Wilson's initial Dominican policy was to give full support to the Constitutional government and at the same time to mediate the differences between it and the rebels. For this task James M. Sullivan, the most notorious "deserving Democrat," was sent to the Republic as American Minister. Sullivan was not equipped to manage the subtleties of Wilson's policy, however, and alienated all parties by failing to keep promises that he had not been authorized to make in the first place.[30]

In the meantime, the Dominicans had scheduled elections for April of 1914. Consistent with the policy of promoting

---

[29]Munro. Dollar Diplomacy. pp. 269-271.

[30]*Ibid*. pp. 277-279.

democracy and the election of "good men" the United States imposed election supervisors on the Republic. In what the supervisors reported as a fair election, Juan Isidro Jiménez was elected to the Dominican presidency. Political and financial chaos continued, nevertheless, and the United States began insisting that the Republic accept a financial adviser having final authority over all budgetary matters. It was further insisted that a national constabulary officered by Americans be organized. Neither Jiménez nor any other Dominican political leader would accept these terms and Wilson would not compromise. On November 19, 1916, American marines occupied the country and established a military government that was to last for eight years.[31]

Intervention, while it resulted from Wilson's convictions concerning America's obligation to promote democratic government in the unhappy Republic, was not a clearly defined goal of his Dominican policy from the beginning. Intervention resulted from a lack of understanding on the part of Wilson and his principal advisers of the conditions existing in the Republic and of its culture and history. Moreover, no policy had ever been formulated to define how far the United States was prepared to go in order to achieve its purposes. Distracted by events in Europe, too little attention was given to the ultimate consequences of the several measures taken in response to circumstances as they arose in the Republic. No preconceived

---

[31]Welles. Naboth's Vineyard. II. Chaps. XII and XIII. pp. 701-796.

line of action was ever formulated and the end result--military intervention--was distasteful to Wilson. By 1916, however, the situation was so far out of control that no alternative was left to him.[32]

Munro has suggested that a partial explanation of the intervention was the suspicion on the part of the Wilson administration that German agents were attempting to influence developments in the Dominican Republic.[33] It is difficult to see just how Germany may have used the troubled country for its own purposes. The German goal may have been merely to distract the United States. It is true that a minimal number of troops--never more than 8,000--were kept out of the European War. These numbers were so inconsequential, however, that it would scarcely have seemed worth the effort. Moreover, the author of this view concedes that Wilson gave greater emphasis to the moral responsibility of the United States to promote constitutional liberty than he did to American defense needs.[34]

Of the occupation itself, little need be said here. The Dominicans did realize some benefits from it. The military government provided eight years of peace in which the country could rehabilitate itself politically and economically.

---

[32] Ibid. pp. 921-922.

[33] Munro. Dollar Diplomacy. p. 270. (Link disputes this view stating that national security was never threatened by events in the Dominican Republic and ". . . played no immediate part . . ." in the policy formulated to meet them. Link. Wilson: The Struggle for Neutrality. (Princeton, N.J., 1960). p. 548)

[34] Ibid. p. 271.

Railroads, highways and schools were built and production of sugar, the country's principal resource, was greatly increased. Balancing these advantages were severe censorship laws and individual acts of violence by marines, mostly in connection with the attempt to suppress bandits in the sparsely populated eastern end of the island. A gulf separated the officers of the military government from the Dominican people, especially after the entrance of the United States into World War I. The occupation authorities lacked training and only rarely did any of them speak Spanish. This compounded misunderstandings which were inevitable in any case. The most important disadvantage of the occupation was the desire of Dominicans to govern themselves, an emotion that no achievement of the military government could offset.[35]

The Dominicans had never expected that the occupation would be more than a temporary expedient. At the close of the World War they began pressuring the Military Governor, Admiral Thomas Snowden, for some indication that it would soon be terminated. Snowden declared publicly that he saw the need for the occupation to continue for at least another twenty years.[36]

At this the Dominican political leaders, Horacio Vásquez, Francisco Reynado, Fedrico Velásquez and others, concluded that only through direct contact with the Department of State could

---

[35]Welles. Naboth's Vineyard. II. pp. 317-321.

[36]Ibid. pp. 816-820.

they hope to bring an early end to the occupation. The State Department had already taken note of the rising chorus of criticism, both in Latin America and at home, of the Dominican occupation and was determined to recapture control over events in the Republic from the military government. As a first step Snowden was directed to appoint a committee of Dominicans nominated by the Department to make recommendations leading to withdrawal of the marines.[37]

The committee met and formulated its recommendations and presented them in December, 1919. The whole effort was wasted, however, when shortly thereafter, Snowden, without authorization, increased the severity of the censorship laws. The Dominicans resigned from the committee and confidence in American intentions was shattered for a time. This incident also provided the radical Union Nacional Dominicana, an extremist organization demanding unconditional withdrawal, with the opportunity to gain a temporary ascendancy over the moderate elements favoring a negotiated evacuation. The State Department was unable to restore the lost confidence of influential Dominicans until the summer of 1921.[38]

The Wilson administration made one more effort to terminate the occupation. On December 24, 1920, a proclamation of evacuation was issued calling for the formation of a new commission to negotiate the terms of withdrawal. The Dominicans, however,

---

[37] Ibid. p. 824.

[38] Ibid. p. 830-834.

were waiting for the inauguration of the new administration in Washington before committing themselves.[39]

The principles guiding the Dominican policy of the Harding administration and the pertinent details of the negotiations leading to withdrawal of the marines are more properly a concern of succeeding chapters. Suffice it to say at this point that a new proclamation of evacuation was enuciated on June 14, 1921, and was more specific than Wilson's had been. It provided the basis for the final agreement on the withdrawal. No agreement was reached, however, until the summer of 1922, when the patient and conciliatory efforts of Sumner Welles, who had been appointed Commissioner to negotiate with the Dominican political leaders, finally won the Dominicans over to an evacuation settlement satisfactory to both parties. Even when terms had been agreed upon, it was not until July 12, 1924, that the military occupation was actually terminated.

---

[39]*Ibid*. p. 835.

CHAPTER II

LEAVING THE SHORES OF SANTO DOMINGO

The Customs Convention of 1924, supplanting the Convention of 1907, paved the way for the withdrawal of the American Marines and the return of self-government to the Dominican Republic. Taken together, these measures reflected the determination of Charles Evans Hughes, Secretary of State from 1921-1925, to discover better means by which to serve the economic and political interests of the United States in the western hemisphere. In light of this, a review of the general considerations guiding Hughes in formulating a Latin American policy will be useful.

The chief innovation in the hemispheric policy of the United States introduced by Hughes was a clarification of the scope and intent of the Monroe Doctrine. Often and publicly between 1921 and 1928, Hughes argued that intervention by the United States in the internal affairs of other American republics could not find justification in the Monroe Doctrine. In so arguing, Hughes did not intend to surrender the presumed right of the United States to intervene when its interests dictated that course. Indeed, he made it clear that this was not his intent--that intervention could be justified on other grounds. While denying that intervention could be legitimized by appealing to the Monroe Doctrine but defending intervention when undertaken on other grounds, Hughes asserted at the same time that American policies were not interventionist but in fact had been aimed at promoting the peaceful development of the hemisphere and especially of the Caribbean republics.

This understanding of the scope and intent of the Monroe Doctrine, muddied though it is by diplomatic casuistry, reveals as fully as anything can Hughes' thinking on Latin American policy. And, as will be shown below, it also provides the foundation for Hoover's Latin American policy. Therefore, it is worth looking at this clarification of Monroe's hallowed pronouncement in some detail.

In an address before the American Bar Association in 1923, Hughes stated that the Monroe Doctrine was in the twentieth century just what it had been in the nineteenth. It was a policy of self-defense aimed at preventing attempts by any non-American power to establish any new colonies in the western hemisphere or to interfere in the affairs of the American republics in any manner that would impair their sovereignty.[1] This position adopted by the United States in 1823 reflected the convictions of American leaders going back to the earliest days of the republic. It was a conviction as deeply held one hundred years later. "It is a policy," Hughes asserted,

> . . . declared by the Executive of the United States and repeated in one form and another by Presidents and Secretaries of State in the conduct of our foreign relations. Its significance lies in the fact that in its essentials . . . it has been for one hundred years and continues to be, an integral part of our national thought and purpose expressing a profound conviction which even the upheaval caused

---

[1]Charles Evans Hughes. "Observations on the Monroe Doctrine." American Journal of International Law (XVII, 1923) p. 612.

> by the Great War . . . has not uprooted or fundamentally changed.[2]

The Monroe Doctrine, Hughes reassured his audience, did not set the stage for an aggressive hemispheric policy by the United States. To the contrary, it had been enunciated in the first place to protect republican institutions in the western hemisphere. Conveniently ignoring the role of the British Navy as the chief enforcer of the doctrine in its early perilous days, Hughes asserted that the United States, partly because of the Monroe Doctrine, had won security for those institutions. Now, he argued, there was no longer a danger from a monarchical old world to the independence and republican character of the American states. Latin American critics, he said, now fear that the real threat to their independence comes from this northern neighbor and that the Monroe Doctrine is the instrument of the prospective tyranny. This was inaccurate, declared Hughes. The Monroe Doctrine provided no such threat to their sovereignty. "Much time has been wasted," he stated,

> . . . in the endeavor to find in the Monroe Doctrine either justification, or the lack of it, for every governmental declaration or action in relation to other American states.[3]

This was a "misconception," Hughes argued, and ". . . a disturbing influence in our relations with Latin American States."[4]

Three months later, in November, 1923, Hughes again

---

[2]<u>Ibid</u>. p. 615.

[3]<u>Ibid</u>. p. 615.

[4]<u>Ibid</u>. p. 617.

addressed himself to this problem and attempted to clear away the "misconception." The Monroe Doctrine, he said, ". . . is a principle of exclusion . . . it aims directly at the exclusion of interposition by non-American powers."[5] The Doctrine was a policy of self-defense on the part of the United States and enforced for its own security. But it had provided "inestimable service" to the Latin American republics. And, far from posing a threat to their sovereignty, the Doctrine ". . . aims to leave the American continents free . . . ."[6] Hughes reiterated this principle in 1928, after he had left the State Department but had been appointed to lead the United States delegation attending the Pan American Conference in Havanna. He criticized those who in the past had pointed to the Monroe Doctrine as an authority legitimizing interference by the United States in the domestic affairs of its American neighbors. This misunderstanding of the Monroe Doctrine, Hughes asserted, had resulted

> . . . in the indulgence in indefinite pronouncements, in making it (Monroe's Doctrine) a cover for extravagant utterances and pretensions which are foreign to the purposes of our government, the demands of our security, and the sentiment of our people. Such statements, implying unwarranted authority of visitation and superintendence, hostile to the proper recognition of the sovereignty of our sister republics, are

---

[5]Charles Evans Hughes. "The Centenary of the Monroe Doctrine." No. 194. <u>International Conciliation</u>. (Greenwich, Conn.: American Association for International Conciliation, 1924) p. 15.

[6]<u>Ibid</u>. p. 14.

> in striking contrast with the carefully measured declaration of Monroe.[7]

In each of these cases, Hughes categorically denied that interventionist policies pursued by previous North American governments found any sanction in the Monroe Doctrine. At the same time, however, he was not prepared to renounce intervention per se. To the contrary, Hughes defended it. It could not be justified by the Monroe Doctrine, Hughes stated in the Bar Association address cited above, but ". . . the Monroe Doctrine as a particular declaration in no way exhausts American right or policy; the United States has rights and obligations which that doctrine does not define."[8] At an earlier point in the address, Hughes explained himself more fully:

> The decision of the question as to what action the United States should take in any exigency arising in this hemisphere is not controlled by the content of the Monroe Doctrine, but may always be determined on grounds of international right and national security as freely as if the Monroe Doctrine did not exist.[9]

The rights and obligations accruing from the concept of national security referred primarily to the Panama Canal and the Caribbean approaches to the canal zone. Hughes was very explicit in his defense of actions aimed at protecting the interests of the United States in these areas. The Panama Canal had created for the United States not only a convenient

---

[7]Charles Evans Hughes. Our Relations to the Nations of the Western Hemisphere. (The Stafford Little Lectures) (Princeton, 1928) p. 17.

[8]Hughes. "Observations on the Monroe Doctrine." p.620.

[9]Ibid. p. 616.

commercial highway but "new exigencies and new conditions of strategy and defense." In the interests of national safety, Hughes declared, the United States

> . . . could not yield to any foreign Power the control of the Panama Canal, or the approaches to it, or the obtaining of any position which would interfere with our right of protection or would menace the freedom of our communications.[10]

In the Caribbean, Hughes claimed for the United States a largely free hand to apply the Monroe Doctrine or any other policy required to safeguard its interests in that area. And the "unsettled condition of certain countries in the region" had made it necessary for the United States to ". . . assert these rights and obligations as well as the limited principles of the Monroe Doctrine."[11]

Hughes readily admitted that Latin Americans resented intervention--or interposition, to use the term he preferred--of any description and "were not disposed to draw distinctions or admit justifications." That he was on the mark is not in doubt. Replying to the Bar Association address, El Nuevo Tiempo of Bogotá editorialized,

> . . . there is nothing more disagreeable than a step-father. Intervention in our internal struggles and protection against European aggression might be regarded in the light of paternal generosity; but history is there to remind us that such altruistic manifestations have served only to humiliate us and

---

[10] *Ibid*. p. 620.

[11] *Ibid*. p. 620.

to deprive us of our legitimate patrimony.[12]

On the other hand, according to Hughes, there were legitimate interests requiring or justifying American interventionist policies. His solution for this dilemma was a discriminatory use of the measure. It should be made clear to Latin Americans precisely what the United States would do and why. "It should be (made) evident," he stated, "that our policy is that of non-intervention; that we limit our interposition to a pressing exigency well established; that we are not seeking control of peoples of other lands or to interfere with governments they desire; that our purposes are reasonable and can readily be justified to governments . . . that perform their admitted international obligations."[13]

The Latin American policy formulated by Hughes affords an interesting contrast to that of the first two decades of the twentieth century. The Roosevelt corollary to the Monroe Doctrine had been renounced. The clearest thing in the many public statements made by Hughes was that intervention--or interposition--could not be undertaken under the aegis of the Monroe Doctrine. But he did not oppose intervention in principle. He defended it, in fact, when what he considered to be the legitimate interests of the United States required it. Needless to say, intervention, whether justified by a sweeping application of the Monroe Doctrine

---

[12]Literary Digest. (Jan. 26, 1924) p. 19. [A review of the response of the Latin American press to both the Bar Association address and the speech commemorating the centennary of the Monroe Doctrine reveals that it was uniformly unfavorable.]

[13]Hughes. "Observations on the Monroe Doctrine." p. 620.

or by some other policy, remained obnoxious to Latin Americans. As pointed out above, even Hughes recognized that hemispheric neighbors would not appreciate the distinction. Some of the American press was equally unfriendly and perceived in it a "diplomatic casuistry."[14]

To the discerning Latin observer, however, Hughes did offer some improvement over the approach taken by the Taft and Wilson administrations. Without labeling it, Hughes did renounce the Taft-Knox Latin American policy known generally as "Dollar Diplomacy." Hughes did not regard it as a responsibility of the American government to take part in or to promote the negotiations of loans and investments by American businessmen in any foreign country including those of Latin America. (Regarding loans, he excepted Cuba, Haiti and the Dominican Republic because of special treaty relations.) It had even less responsibility, Hughes stated, ". . . as to the repayment of amounts borrowed. Nothing could be further from American policy than the suggestion of any assurance by our Government that ordinary contract debts will be collected by force. We never pledge the use of force to collect debts . . . ."[15]

In this, Hughes had removed himself a good distance from the attitude of Philander C. Knox. The latter assumed that what

---

[14]Literary Digest. (February 4, 1928) p. 11. [Quoted from the New York World. Other papers reported as negative are the Cleveland Plain Dealer and Baltimore Sun.]

[15]Hughes. Hemisphere Relations. p. 64.

was good for American business was also good for the nations of the Caribbean. This "pernicious phase" of the Latin American policy of the United States resulted in the latter forcing upon the people of this area governments deemed suitable to the requirements of the American State Department.[16] "Suitable" governments were those able to maintain an orderly atmosphere in which American trade and investment could flourish. Hughes was vigorous in defense of property rights, more so, certainly, than later administrations would be. He was with equal certainty, disinclined to allow that motive to become the prime consideration in the hemispheric relations of the United States.

In quite a different way, Hughes' approach to relations with Latin America represented a departure from that of Wilson's administration. While he defended the right of the United States to intervene, Hughes based that right on what he considered to be the legitimate self-interest of his government. This view was less patronizing than that projected by Wilson. Hughes never considered it a legitimate object of the United States to teach the Latins how to elect "good men."

While Hughes' Latin American policy differed, to a degree at least, from that of Taft and Wilson, it held few innovations. In its broad assumptions his policy was governed by the same motives as Theodore Roosevelt's had been. It was not likely,

---

[16] Welles. Naboth's Vineyard. II. p. 919.

therefore, that the hostility of Latin Americans would be greatly reduced during his tenure at the State Department. Hughes and his Republican successors were fully as cognizant of the need and desirability of improving relations with the other nations of the western hemisphere as was the Roosevelt administration after 1933. The former sought this improvement by a cautious interpretation and application of the right to intervene. They would not renounce that right altogether. Nothing short of this, however, would satisfy the Latin Americans. The subtle changes in United States policy instituted by Hughes and continued more or less until 1932 fell far short of what the Latin Americans, even those who may have taken note of them, desired.

With this general view of the Latin American policy of the 1920's as background, attention can now be directed to its application to the specific situation then existing in the Dominican Republic. Hughes was faced with the immediate task of terminating the military occupation and restoring self-government to the Dominicans. In the process of realizing this end, a new convention was negotiated to replace that of 1907.

The issues that confronted the Hoover administration's Dominican policy in 1930 and 1931 arose out of the relationships created by this convention. To fully understand the reasons behind the negotiation of a new customs convention in 1924 requires a review of the negotiations leading to the withdrawal of the American occupation forces. The modified convention grew out of the need by both the military government, during its tenure, and the Dominican civilian government, when it assumed office, to float new loans. With these increases in the Dominican public debt, and the consequent diversion of a larger portion of the revenue to service it, it became necessary to modify the terms upon which it would be retired. The unpaid balance of the principal of the $20,000,000 loan of 1907 was $7,500,000 and was scheduled to be retired by 1929. With the retirement of the bonds representing this debt the customs receivership was to be terminated. The retirement of the unpaid balance of the bond issue of 1907, by itself, imposed no undue burden on Dominican resources. Had the debt not been increased the receivership very likely would have been closed out according to schedule. Additional loans were made during the occupation, however, and the servicing of these bonds when added to the previous loan did create a strain on Dominican resources. Because of these new loans a new convention, resulting in the extension of the life of the receivership, was negotiated.

The political chaos prevailing in the Dominican Republic from 1911 to 1916 had led to an increase in the public debt and a collapse of sound fiscal administration. As a consequence, President Wilson had demanded prior to the occupation that the Dominican government yield control of its budget to a financial adviser designated by the United States. The military government, upon assuming the direction of Dominican affairs, found it necessary to float a loan in 1918 in order to correct the financial disarray. Not only was it needed to correct the results of past financial practices, but it was desired by the military authorities to aid them in carrying out an ambitious public works program. This loan amounted to $5,000,000 and was secured by customs receipts. It was to be retired by 1925 and would not, therefore, result in the extension of the life of the receivership.[17]

The additional loan did, of course, increase the drain on Dominican revenues. During the post-war economic boom, however, there was no difficulty in meeting this added burden. It was not until the business recession of 1921 that difficulty arose. When revenues were found to be insufficient to meet the service of the debt, pay the ordinary governmental expenses, and provide for the completion of the public works programs, the military government sought approval of yet another loan. At the same time the United States was looking for the quickest way to end the occupation and was reluctant to increase the Dominican debt. The military government had requested approval of a bond issue for $10,000,000 before the Wilson administration had left office. It had been refused then and Hughes rejected the request again after he became Secretary of State. He did, however, approve a $2,500,000 loan on June 21, 1921.

Only one week earlier, on June 14, a new proclamation of

---

[17]U.S. Dept. of State: Papers Relating to the Foreign Relations of the United States. Vol. II. 1922. Washington, D.C., 1938. Financial Report of the Military Governor, Rear-Admiral Samuel S. Robison, 21 Jan. 1922, 839.00/2461. pp. 8-9.

evacuation had been presented to the Dominicans. The proclamation differed from the one of December, 1920, in that it included a step by step program of evacuation and set down the conditions under which the United States would withdraw. One of these stipulations extended the powers of the General Receiver of customs to collect and disburse the internal revenues of the Dominican Republic if customs receipts should prove insufficient to meet the external obligations. Another provided for the extension of the receivership until all the loans made during the occupation were paid in full. The validity of these loans, as well as all other acts of the military government, would be expressly recognized by the new Dominican government before the occupation ended. Relating only indirectly to the negotiation of a new convention were provisions for the training of a Dominican constabulary by American officers and the election of a constitutional government. The United States would assist in supervising these elections and the occupation would end only after the new government had assumed office.[18]

The Dominicans objected at first to the extension of the powers of the General Receiver. Hughes instructed William Russell, long the American Minister at Santo Domingo, to explain to the Dominicans that the loan of $2,500,000 requested by the military government was absolutely necessary if the public works projects already begun were to be completed.

---

[18] _Foreign Relations_. I. 1921. Enclosure from Denby to Hughes, Proclamation of Evacuation: 7 June 1921, 839.00/2395. p. 835.

Owing to international financial conditions then obtaining, it would be necessary to offer added security in the form of internal revenues in case customs receipts did not suffice to the prospective purchasers of the bonds. Russell was to assure them that such powers would probably never be used.[19] By August 3, 1921, Admiral Robison could report that he had reached agreement with influential Dominicans regarding extension of the powers and duties of the General Receiver.[20]

There were other terms of the evacuation that they would not accept, however. In an earlier report Robison had disclosed that Federico Velásquez, leader of the Progresista Party and, at this time, a close political ally of the influential and popular Horacio Vásquez, had raised two objections to the American plan of evacuation. The first of these concerned the conflicts that might arise after the proposed elections when a Dominican constitutional government would exist alongside the military government for an undetermined length of time. The Dominicans insisted that when their own elected government took office the military government and occupation must have terminated. Secondly, Velásquez was unalterably opposed to the provision for the continued training of the Dominican constabulary

---

[19]Ibid. Hughes to Russell. 28 June 1921, 839.00/2408a. p. 840. [Russell had been the United States Minister to the Republic throughout the period of military occupation. The military government had been recognized as the legitimate Dominican government by the United States and Nicaragua.]

[20]Ibid. Denby (Sec. of the Navy) to Hughes, Robison's Confidential Report, 25 August 1921, 839.00/2459. p. 840.

by American officers once independence was restored. If Velásquez objected to any of the proposals concerning the status of the customs receivership and other financial matters, Robison failed to mention them.[21]

As stated previously, Hughes had approved a $2,500,000 loan requested by the military government. Although not officially authorized until June 21, 1921, approval had been granted by June 1. This loan had been accounted for in the evacuation proclamation of June 14, and fell under that paragraph relating to the extension of the powers of the General Receiver and was thus secured by the customs and internal revenues of the Republic. As was the case with the 1918 loan, this loan was to be retired by 1925. The military government was not satisfied and renewed its request for approval of an additional $7,500,000. This, along with the loan of $2,500,000 already approved, would total the $10,000,000 requested in 1920. The purpose of the loan was to retire the two previous loans of 1918 and 1921, totaling at that time approximately $4,000,000 and leaving enough to complete the public works program and a working balance of $2,000,000.[22]

Hughes rejected the request on December 23, 1921, contending that a loan of this size would interfere with the plans for an early withdrawal of the occupation forces. It would not be

---

[21] Ibid. Russell to Hughes. Robison Report. 5 November 1921, 839.00/2450. p. 851.

[22] Ibid. Hughes to Herod. (American charge at Santo Domingo). 23 Dec. 1921. 839.51/2240. pp. 866-867.

consistent with the terms of the evacuation proclamation and would indicate a lack of good faith on the part of the United States. He believed also that sufficient funds were available for ordinary governmental expenses and the completion of public works projects already begun. In his judgment no new programs should be initiated until independence had been restored to the Republic. Moreover, Hughes wrote that he did not see any possibility that so large a bond issue would be purchased at that time, especially since it was known that the United States intended soon to withdraw its military forces. Finally, he opposed the loan because it would entail the prolongation of the receivership. Previous loans had not had this effect. To do so now would complicate the plans for withdrawal of the occupation forces.[23]

Had the Dominican political leadership cooperated, it is probable that this loan would not have been approved--unless requested by the Dominican government. This, as it happened, was one of the reasons the Dominicans were uncooperative. They were, as well, suspicious of every conciliatory effort by the United States. Much of this hostility stemmed from the impolitic conduct of Admiral Snowden during his tenure as Military Governor. It was also the result of the propaganda of an extreme nationalist group, the Union Nacional Dominicana, led by Federico Henríquez y Carvajal, provisional president in 1916 at

---

[23]Ibid. p. 866.

the time of the military intervention. This radical group intimidated the leaders of other parties and accused them of treason if they surrendered to any of the terms of the proclamation of June 14. The solution they proposed was for the United States to withdraw unconditionally and restore the status quo ante. Among other things, this meant placing Henríquez in the presidency. The Dominicans would then settle their own domestic difficulties.[24]

As a consequence, no Dominican leader of influence could sit down to negotiate the terms of evacuation and remain influential--not, at least, until the strong sentiment agitated by the nacionalistas had subsided. From the standpoint of those Dominicans with political aspirations it was better to allow the occupation to continue than to become identified with a negotiated withdrawal. Hughes' efforts were unavailing and slight progress was made during the summer and fall of 1921.[25]

It had become quite apparent, as the year 1922 opened, that a new approach to evacuation would have to be devised. One feature of any new plan, it was realized, would be the extension of the occupation beyond its originally scheduled termination. Since it was apparently inevitable that the military government would be extended, Hughes was compelled to revise his earlier opinion regarding a large, long-term loan.

---

[24]Welles. Naboth's Vineyard. II. pp. 850-851.

[25]Ibid. p. 851.

On January 30, 1922, Secretary of the Navy Denby authorized the military government to enter into negotiations for a $10,000,000 loan. This was a preliminary step to determine whether Dominican bonds, if offered, would be purchased. In a note to Hughes explaining this action, Denby argued for the need of "permanent" financing. In his view it would be necessary for the Dominican government during the foreseeable future to finance their operations by long term borrowing. Financing of this type would provide for the development of the country at a pace and on a scale not possible if dependent on Dominican revenues only. For the present and foreseeable future at least, a share of these revenues would necessarily have to be pledged as security for the loans. Denby did not attempt to obscure the fact that this would necessitate the extension of the life of the receivership. He did point out, however, that the loan then under study, if not made by the military government, would be an immediate necessity for a native Dominican government upon resuming direction of national affairs. The only way the Dominicans could float such a loan would be to agree to the extension of the receivership.[26]

Denby's note to Hughes could only have been his résumé of tentative decisions reached during conversations with the Secretary of State and/or other officers of the Department. The State Department was in complete control of Dominican policy

---

[26]Foreign Relations. II. 1922 Denby to Hughes. 30 Jan. 1922. 839.00/2461. pp. 5-6.

and Denby could not have authorized the military government to initiate loan negotiations without prior approval from Hughes. Furthermore, implicit in the authorization to negotiate with the bankers was the assurance that if the bonds were purchased on reasonable terms the $10,000,000 loan would be approved.

Denby made a further recommendation in this same note. He urged that Admiral Robison and Russell arrange for another conference with Dominican political leaders. If they did not agree to the terms of the evacuation proclamation, he proposed that it be withdrawn until the public works projects and the training of a constabulary were completed.[27] Hughes was not then prepared to go that far. He still hoped that the Dominicans would agree to a modified version of the proclamation of June 14. On February 10, 1922, he instructed Russell to call the Dominican leaders to a conference to attempt to get their approval of the $10,000,000 loan. He made it clear that the loan would be authorized in any case but he preferred to obtain the tacit approval of the Dominicans as might be expressed by their participation in the elections provided for in the plan for evacuation.[28]

These elections had been scheduled for July, 1921, but the Dominican political parties had refused to participate and

---

[27]Ibid. p. 5.

[28]Ibid. Hughes to Russell. 19 Feb. 1922. 839.00/2462. p. 12.

the elections had been postponed. Russell was to discuss the matter with them ". . . with the utmost frankness."[29] He was to explain that the loan was essential to complete the public works program and to refund the loans of 1918 and 1921. The latter could be accomplished quite advantageously under the existing market conditions if done before May 1, 1922. This was the reason for urging immediate action. Russell was also to explain that the loan was absolutely essential to the financial stability and economic development of the country. If not made by the military government it would subsequently have to be made by a Dominican government. The necessity for extending the duration of the receivership was to be explained in equally frank terms.[30]

In order to obtain an expression of approval of the loan by Dominicans, Hughes was willing to make two concessions regarding the terms of evacuation. First, the Dominicans could supervise their own election should one materialize. Secondly, the United States would not insist upon a military mission being sent to the Republic to recruit and train the constabulary. It would require only that a legation guard remain in Santo Domingo after evacuation until public order was sufficiently established by a constabulary officered by Dominicans. Also an agreement might be made, if so desired by the

---

[29] Ibid. p. 12.

[30] Ibid. p. 11.

Dominicans, by which the officers of the legation guard would serve as instructors in the Dominican constabulary.[31] On March 5, Russell reported that he and Robison had called the conference of Dominican leaders per instructions. He wrote that,

> It seemed that all of those attending the conference came with their minds made up to accept nothing, as very little attention was paid to our statement. . . .[32]

Their principal objection, he continued, was to the plan for the legation guard and ". . . nothing whatever was said in regard to the financial plan . . . ." Russell believed that the Dominicans found the plan of permanent financing perfectly acceptable, ". . . but the responsibility therefore has been evaded."[33] Later that same day, in their joint reply to these overtures, the Dominican leaders stated that, ". . . it is impossible to consider any point raised in the conference."[34] This could have meant exactly what it said, of course, and if so, it was a rejection of those terms of the evacuation relating to loans and the prolongation of the receivership. It must be kept in mind, howevever, that this statement was made for public consumption.

Later negotiations regarding the evacuation tend to

---

[31]Ibid. p. 11.

[32]Ibid. Russell to Hughes. 5 Mar. 1922. 839.00/2479. p. 13.

[33]Ibid. p. 14.

[34]Ibid. Enclosure of Russell's dispatch. p. 17.

confirm Russell's judgment. Admiral Robison certainly concurred with him. In his January report he had stated that he did not believe the Dominicans would agree to participate in elections unless a large loan was floated. In his view, without such a loan Dominican finances would be in such disarray that no aspiring politician would want to take charge of the country.[35]

Upon this rejection of the plan for evacuation, modified as it was, Hughes was forced to give up the idea of an early withdrawal. If the Dominicans could not be convinced to permit the completion of projects, deemed by the United States to be essential, after they had resumed control of their own government, then these ends would have to be achieved before the occupation was terminated. With this in mind, Robison was instructed to withdraw the proclamations of evacuation of June 14, 1921, and December 23, 1920. At the same time he was to announce that the military occupation would continue until the public works program was completed and a national constabulary had been established. Furthermore, after these projects had been completed, withdrawal would depend on the formation of a constitutional Dominican government and on the negotiation of a convention of evacuation stipulating the extension of the life of the customs receivership until the $10,000,000 loan of 1922 had been retired.[36]

---

[35]Ibid. Report of the Military Governor in: Denby to Hughes, 30 Jan. 1922. 839.00/2461. p. 7.

[36]Ibid. Proclamation of the Military Governor, 6 Mar. 1922. 839.00/2528. pp. 18019.

Paradoxically, the Dominican leadership achieved nearly all that it desired when the proclamation of evacuation was withdrawn. As evidence of this Federico Velásquez, with assurances of cooperation from other party leaders, particularly from Horacio Vásquez, sought out Russell and stated that when finances were in order as a result of the loan and the constabulary was of sufficient strength to secure public order without the continued supervision of American officers, then he and his colleagues would make proposals regarding elections preparatory to the withdrawal of the occupation forces. Velásquez recognized, Russell reported, that these two essentials, the loan and the establishment of the national police, were ". . . absolutely necessary preliminaries to electing native government. . . ."[37]

During the negotiations that proceeded from March through August of 1922, both in Washington and Santo Domingo, culminating in the signing of a Convention of Evacuation on September 12, 1922, no direct mention was made of the loans or the extension of the life of the receivership. They were not subjects for negotiation. With regard to the formation of their government and the training and officering of a constabulary the Dominican demands were met in full. They made no substantive demands regarding the receivership. First, they recognized that the United States would not agree to any convention of

---

[37]Ibid. Russell to Hughes. 28 Mar. 1922. 839.00/2499. p. 19.

evacuation that did not include recognition of the debt incurred during the occupation and that the receivership would continue until all bonds outstanding were fully redeemed. Secondly, the Dominicans themselves recognized the need for the loans and had not expressed opposition to the prolongation of the receivership as a prerequisite to their approval. The Dominicans had at an earlier date objected to the extension of the powers and duties of the General Receiver to collect and disburse Dominican internal revenues. This was no longer an issue, however. International financial conditions had improved. More importantly, the $10,000,000 loan was to be repaid over a longer period and not to be fully retired until 1942. There was no foreseeable danger that customs receipts would prove insufficient to service this debt. The first payment on the principal was not due until 1930.

Throughout these negotiations the Dominicans requested only two changes in the Convention of Evacuation relating to financial matters, and these were minor. They reveal, nevertheless, the two most important reasons for the ultimate negotiation of the new Customs Convention of 1924. The Dominican Commissioners wanted it understood that the United States would raise no objection to an eventual agreement with bondholders modifying the terms of the retirement of the 1922 loan. An understanding of this nature was desired, first, because the Dominican Commissioners did not want it to appear to their constituents that approval by the United States Senate was required to effect such changes should they prove necessary or desirable; secondly, and quite simply, they did not want to be prevented from making these changes should some advantage in doing so present itself. Sumner Welles, United States Commissioner to the Dominican Republic, agreed that both sides understood this to be the case, but no stipulation to this effect was incorporated into the Evacuation Convention.[38]

A second point the Dominicans regarded as unclear pertained to the limitations placed on their freedom to modify Dominican tariffs by Executive Order No. 735. This decree issued by the military government had authorized the issuance of the 1922 bonds. It included a paragraph which, in effect, stated that as long as any of the bonds of that loan remained outstanding, the Dominican tariff could not be modified without the prior consent of the United States. The Dominicans requested only that the Evacuation Convention clearly stipulute that modifications of the tariff were governed by the terms of the 1907 Customs Convention: the tariff could be altered by agreement between the executives of both nations if it could be demonstrated that, had such changes occurred two years previously, the customs receipts for that two year period would still have been in excess of $2,000,000. Welles regarded this as a superfluous addition to the Convention but agreed, nevertheless, to include it in the instrument. It pleased the Dominicans and in no way affected the purposes of the United States.[39]

---

[38]Ibid. Welles to Hughes. 2 Sept. 1922. 839.00/2584. p. 49.

[39]Ibid. p. 49.

While nothing was said concerning a revision of the Convention of 1907 during the negotiations leading to evacuation, the Dominican proposals regarding adjustment of the amortization payments and tariff modification anticipated precisely the two most significant changes made in the new Customs Convention negotiated in 1924 to replace the Treaty of 1907. When discussions for revision of the 1907 Convention came, however, the United States took the initiative, not the Dominicans. The new convention was proposed to remove the aggravations resulting from the drain on Dominican revenues created by the demanding schedule of payments on the outstanding bonds and the restrictions on Dominican sovereignty regarding tariff modification. The purpose in initiating these negotiations was threefold. First, it was hoped that some financial relief might be gained for the Dominican Republic. Secondly, these modifications were designed to improve the image of the United States not only in the Dominican Republic but throughout Latin America. Finally, the interests of American investors and merchants were safeguarded.

The occasion for making the proposal was the visit of Horacio Vásquez, Dominican President-elect, to the United States in June, 1924. Sumner Welles had urged that Vásquez be received as the official guest of the American government. He argued that the standing policy of the United States opposing this practice be disregarded in this instance due to the special relationship existing between the two nations.[40] Hughes declined this suggestion. He did arrange, however, for Vásquez to be accorded military honors by the War Department and to receive courtesies from President Coolidge at a White House luncheon.[41]

Welles further advised that Vásquez would be accompanied by José del Carmen Ariza, who was to be appointed Dominican Minister to Washington by Vásquez after his inauguration in August. Their purpose in wanting to visit Washington was to discuss the possibility of floating a refunding loan which would require approval by the State Department. Welles explained that a new loan would enable the Dominican government ". . . to obtain a larger portion of the customs revenues for current expenses . . . ."[42] It was hoped that this could be achieved by spreading amortization of the debt over a longer period. It must have become apparent to the Department by this time that this method of diverting a larger share of the receipts to the Dominican government had reached a point of diminishing returns.

The Dominican debt, even excluding the 1907 loan to be fully retired in 1929, was in excess of $10,000,000. To add

---

[40] For. Rel. I. 1924. Welles to Hughes. 16 May 1924. 839.00/2833. p. 627.

[41] Acting Secretary Joseph C. Grew to the President. 17 June 1924. 033.3911/7a; and, Grew to the Secretary of War. 18 June 1924. 033.3911/7b.

[42] *Ibid*. Welles to Hughes. 16 May 1924. 839.00/2833. p. 627.

to it now would make it virtually impossible to lower the annual service charges of interest and amortization to the extent necessary to achieve the desired result. Article one of the Convention of 1907 stipulated that one-twelfth of the annual charges for interest and amortization--totaling $100,000--was to be withheld from customs receipts each month before the Dominican government received anything. On a yearly basis this totaled $1,200,000. To this was now added the interest on the 1922 loan. Another feature of Article one was the provision for remittance to the sinking fund of fifty per cent of all receipts over $3,000,000. The only possibility of diverting more of the revenue derived from customs to the Dominican government lay in the modification of this feature of the 1907 Treaty.

Although no suggestion of this nature was made to the Dominican government prior to Vásquez' arrival in Washington, that it had been under consideration in the Department is revealed in a memorandum prepared on June 19, 1924, concerning matters to be discussed with the Dominican President-elect. First on this list was revision of the 1907 Treaty. Moreover, a complete draft of the proposed new Convention had been prepared. This draft was to be presented to Vásquez as the basis for negotiations.[43]

The draft of the new Convention differed from the Treaty of 1907 in four important respects. In the preamble it provided

---

[43]State Department Memo. June 19, 1924. 033.3911/14.

for the flotation of additional loans up to $25,000,000. While this amounted to tacit recognition of the Dominican need to float additional loans, Article three of the Convention provided the United States with the means necessary to prevent the issuance of bonds for all or any part of the amount stipulated in the preamble. Article three of the new Convention was identical to the provision of the 1907 Convention: the Dominican Republic could not increase its public debt without the consent of the United States. A new Article six was added providing for the arbitration of disputes arising over any of the provisions of the Convention. The scope of the arbitral tribunal and, of course, the tribunal itself, was to be determined in each individual case as it arose.[44]

Of greater significance were the revisions of Articles one and four, relating respectively to the terms of payment of the loans and the modification of the Dominican tariff. Article one of the draft provided that a sum equal to one-twelfth of the annual charges for interest and amortization of the outstanding bonds would be withheld from the customs receipts each month by the General Receiver. Except for phraseology this was the same as provided in the existing Convention. In the last paragraph of the first article, however, it was stipulated that only ten per cent of the annual collections over $4,000,000 need be applied to the sinking fund for retirement

---

[44]Copy of the Draft Convention in State Dept. Memo cited in footnote 32.

of bonds. From the Dominican point of view this represented a substantial improvement over the restrictive nature of the Convention of 1907.[45]

Another major concession made by the United States is found in Article four. It will be recalled that the Convention of 1907 required the consent of the United States prior to the modification of the tariff. It could not be altered at all unless it could be shown that, if the modified rates had been in effect during the two preceding years, the customs receipts for that period would have amounted to at least $2,000,000. In the draft of the proposed new convention, the requirement of approval by the United States was deleted. It was merely stipulated that the Dominican government agreed not to modify its tariff to such an extent that customs collections would be reduced to amounts less than one and one-half times the sum needed for servicing its public debt based on the application of the desired altered rates to the importations of the preceding two years.[46]

This concession was not made without exacting something in return. On the list of matters to be discussed with Vásquez was a proposal for an exchange of notes between the two governments effecting a most favored nation treatment of each other's exports. In this case also a draft of the notes proposed to be

---

[45] Ibid.

[46] Ibid.

exchanged had been prepared. The most favored nation treatment was to apply to all commodities with the important exception of certain Cuban agricultural products. Of principal concern to Dominicans was Cuban sugar. Since 1902, the United States had granted a twenty per cent preferential tariff rate to Cuban sugar. This preference was provided for by treaty and could not have been changed readily even had there been a desire to do so.[47]

Dominican sugar, the country's largest export item, could not compete with the Cuban product on the American market. The Dominicans, therefore, looked to Canadian and Western European markets for its buyers. They suffered under the constant fear that these would be closed to them also as more countries worked out special arrangements for acquiring sugar. In 1922, Welles had reported on the proceedings of a meeting of the Dominican Chamber of Commerce during which complaints were uttered concerning this handicap. The Dominicans decried the fact that they could not modify their tariffs without permission from the United States. This precluded any possibility of their arranging reciprocity agreements with nations other than the United States by which they might ensure markets for their sugar and other commodities in return for granting tariff preferences to the manufactures of those countries. The United States demanded equal treatment for the products it exported to the Dominican Republic but would not grant to Dominican agricultural goods,

---

[47]Ibid.

principally sugar, treatment equal to that accorded to Cuban products.[48]

Perhaps Hughes had this in mind when he explained to President Coolidge the need for the proposed most favored nation agreement. In preparation for the Vásquez visit he wrote to the President that one of the Dominican hopes was to get consent to modify its tariff schedule. If this were permitted, it was very possible that British and other European imports to the Republic would be given preferential duties over competing American products. The purpose of such a step would be to secure markets for Dominican sugar. The United States, he continued, could refuse to permit the desired tariff revision since, according to the terms of the Convention of 1907, this was its prerogative. This, he wrote, was not a desirable procedure. He emphasized that if the United States retained this option, the Dominican Republic would be reminded constantly of the external authority exercised over its commerce and finance. He concluded that American trade and commerce could be protected adequately against discriminatory tariffs by the proposed most favored nation agreement, a method commonly practiced among sovereign nations.[49]

W.R. McClure, of the Economic Advisor's Office, submitted a proposal intended to offset the exception of Cuban sugar from

---

[48]Welles to Hughes. 10 Sept. 1922. 611.3931/16.

[49]For. Rel. I. Hughes to Coolidge. 20 June 1924. 611.3931/8a. p. 666.

the agreement. He made the "very tentative" suggestion that the Dominican Republic be permitted to except its trade with Haiti from the proposed unconditional most favored nation treatment to be granted to the United States. Welles replied that such a proposal would not be well received by the Dominicans. First, he wrote, there was no commerce at all between the two countries. Secondly, in reference to the traditional enmity between the two countries, he pointed out that there were "special reasons" why the Dominicans would not welcome this "concession."[50]

Whatever bargaining the Dominicans might have attempted regarding this agreement is not revealed in the State Department records. Apparently, no memoranda exist of the conversations held at Washington during the Vásquez visit. Moreover, there is no trace of correspondence concerning the most favored nation agreement until September 6, 1924, at which time Ariza, the Dominican Minister at Washington, received instructions authorizing him to enter into an exchange of notes concluding the agreement. Indeed, Ariza did not even have a copy of the text of the agreement and had to ask the Department to supply him with one.[51] The exchange of notes putting the most favored nation agreement into force took place on September 27, 1924. The text was identical to that of the draft presented to Vásquez

---

[50]McClure to Welles and the latter's reply. 18 June 1924. 611.3931/7.

[51]Memo by Dana G. Munro of Conversation with Jose del Carmen Ariza. 6 Sept. 1924. 611.3931/15.

in the preceding June.[52]

There are likewise no memoranda of the exchanges of views that might have taken place during the Vásquez visit concerning the revised Customs Convention. There were, however, active negotiations over certain of its features after Vásquez was inaugurated on July 12, 1924. The Dominicans did not seek to improve advantages already gained regarding the easing of the terms of payment of the loans and the removal of some of the restrictions pertaining to tariff modification. These stood as proposed in the June draft.

The attempt by Vásquez to gain further concessions on other features of the Convention was, as much as anything else, an effort to untrack his domestic opposition. His overwhelming electoral victory in March had been, in part, a result of a coalition with Velásquez's Progresista Party. Velásquez had been elected to the vice-presidency on the same ticket. After the inauguration the coalition began to disintegrate and Velásquez's party led the opposition to the Convention as an indication of its mood. After the Convention had been signed and laid before the Dominican Senate for its approval, William Russell reported to the Department that opposition to it had subsided because Velásquez had been shown more consideration by Vásquez. Velásquez had told Russell that previously Vásquez had rejected his advice and had been unfair to his party's claims

---

[52]*For. Rel.* I. 1924. Draft of the most favored nation agreement. pp. 666-667.

for offices.[53]

Orme Wilson of the Latin American Division of the State Department conveyed this information to Sumner Welles who, according to Wilson, thought this an inaccurate account of the situation. According to Wilson, Welles believed that,

> . . . Velásquez has been making trouble in order to prevent the approval of the Convention by the Dominican Congress and thereby force Vásquez to resign. He could then succeed and would negotiate a new convention substantially similar to the one now under consideration which he would expect to put into effect and reap all the glory for himself.[54]

Welles did not believe that Vasqùez had any intention of permitting this to happen.[55]

The Dominican government seemed to have no clear conception of precisely what changes it desired and thought were attainable. It pressed for one modification until it was rejected and then, at the eleventh hour, put forward a different proposal. It first pressed for a modification of Article three, which stipulated that until the outstanding bonds had been fully redeemed, the Dominican ". . . public debt shall not be increased except by previous agreement . . ." between the two governments.[56] On November 8, 1924 the Dominican government proposed that the word "contractually" be inserted after

---

[53]Russell to Hughes. 11 Feb. 1925. 839.51/2528.

[54]Note attached to Russell dispatch cited in footnote 47 above. Summary by Orme Wilson of remarks made by Welles.

[55]_Ibid_.

[56]See Appendix II. Article three of the Convention.

"increased" and before "except."[57]

The Dominicans apparently hoped that by specifying that only a contractual increase of the public debt required the consent of the United States, the terms of the Convention would be sufficiently vague to allow them to increase the debt by issuing domestic bonds. All governments, of course, have a "floating" debt incurred by the issuance of short-term notes or bonds designed to meet current obligations. The Dominican government was no exception. The Dominicans had something more than this in mind, however. They apparently hoped to be able to maintain a floating debt represented by government bonds not redeemable during the fiscal year in which they were issued. This was a device practiced by Vásquez later, even without the desired change in the Convention. Under Trujillo this practice was carried to absurd lengths.

In 1924, the Department response was not a rude "no," but it was "no" just the same. It agreed to a slight modification, but one that was even less open to interpretation than the words of the original draft. By the wording suggested in the Department's reply, the Dominican government could ". . . not incur additional national obligations to which the credit of the Nation . . . (was) pledged . . ." except with the consent of the United States.[58] If the term "public debt" was vague as to

[57]Russell to Hughes. 8 Nov. 1924. 839.51/2485.

[58]Hughes to Russell. 26 Nov. 1924. 839.51/2485.

whether it meant foreign or internal debt or both, the term "national obligation" would seem to have left no room for doubt. Nevertheless, Ariza visited the Department a few days later and replied that this too was acceptable if the word "contractually" could be inserted between "non" and "incur."[59]

When, ultimately, this was rejected, the Dominicans preferred the wording of the original draft. Before conceding the point, however, Ariza explained to Francis White, Assistant Secretary, that it would strengthen the Vásquez government politically if it could be shown that it had been able to get some concession from the United States. White predicted that due to noisy opposition to Vásquez, it would be difficult for him to concede this point.[60]

White was proved incorrect in this instance. On December 10, Ariza was instructed to suspend discussions on Article three and to seek a change in Article one. It was this article of the Convention that had been modified to ease the terms of payment of the loans and to divert a greater share of customs revenue to the Dominican government. Another paragraph of the article provided for the appointment of the General Receiver of Customs and his assistants. It was this section of Article one that the Dominicans now wanted modified.[61]

---

[59]Memo by Francis White of conversation with Ariza. 2 Dec. 1924. 839.51/2494.

[60]<u>Ibid</u>.

[61]Memo by Orme Wilson of conversation with Ariza. 10 Dec. 1924. 839.51/2495.

The United States, since the conclusion of the 1907 Convention, had interpreted this paragraph of Article one to mean that power had been delegated by the President of the United States to the General Receiver to appoint and discharge the personnel of the customs service engaged in handling the collection of revenues. The Dominican government, for its part, had argued that these powers did not apply to personnel appointed in accordance with Dominican laws. A serious dispute over these conflicting interpretations had arisen in 1907. The dispute centered around the "interventores," the appraisers of merchandise appointed by the Dominican government. William Pulliam, the General Receiver, insisted that these customs officers must be subject to his discipline and, if corrupt or inefficient, be dismissed. Secretary of State Root suggested that Pulliam and the Dominican government get together on the appointments and dismissals of personnel to these posts. It was to the best advantage of both parties if they could effect an amicable agreement. This had been the approach taken to the issue since 1907.[62]

In 1924, however, the Dominicans proposed to incorporate this working agreement into the treaty. For the future, it was proposed specifically that the views of the Dominican President should be considered in the matter of appointments and dismisals. The proposal was rejected promptly, firmly and without

---

[62]Welles. Naboth's Vineyard. pp. 659-660.

any alternative suggestion.[63] The next day, December 18, Hughes instructed Russell to inform the Dominican government that no proposition limiting the authority of the General Receiver in the efficient performance of his duties would be entertained. The instruction continued,

> You will please inform President Vásquez of the Department's views and say that the Department would regret any obstacle to the prompt conclusion of the Convention such as would be caused by the submission now after several months negotiations of further proposals to make important changes in the text of the proposed convention . . . .[64]

It was clear from this that nothing was to be gained by further delay. Even before this instruction was sent the Dominican government had yielded on all points. On December 17, Russell reported that he had seen Ariza's powers to sign the Convention as it had been proposed in June.[65] Ariza brought his authorization to sign to the Department on December 22, and, after a few days delay to correct the English and Spanish texts, the Convention was signed on December 27, 1924.[66]

The United States Senate, in an unusual display of deliberate speed where a treaty was concerned, gave its consent on January 21, 1925, less than a month after the Convention had been submitted.[67] The Dominican Senate proved much less pliable.

---

[63]Memo by Wilson of conversation with Ariza. 17 Dec. 1924. 839.51/2498.

[64]Hughes to Russell. 18 Dec. 1924. 839.51/2496.

[65]Russell to Hughes. 17 Dec. 1924. 839.51/2496.

[66]White memo to Hughes. 22 Dec. 1924. 839.51/2496.

[67]Hughes to Ariza. 24 Jan. 1924. 839.51/2516a.

With the signing of the Convention the opposition to Vásquez united in an effort to bring about his political demise. As early as January 23, Russell had warned that opposition from the Dominican Congress and press would be determined.[68] A few days later found him less pessimistic and he dismissed the opponents of the Convention as misguided nationalists. He recalled that the current agitation was ". . . exactly what took place in 1907 prior to the ratification of the Convention."[69]

The center of the opposition was once again Federico Velásquez. Welles approached him about his role in obstructing the Convention. He reminded Velásquez that he had supported the new Convention prior to the withdrawal of the American Marines and expressed surprise that he now opposed it. Velasquez explained that he was not opposed to the Convention but only to the part of it providing for the flotation of loans amounting to $25,000,000. He believed that the proceeds of these loans would be expended unwisely by distributing them to local governments.[70]

Velásquez also evinced displeasure with the emerging influence of José de Alfonseca. This Dominican had risen to become the principal adviser near Vásquez. Velásquez regarded him as a schemer who had undermined his influence with the

---

[68]Russell to Hughes. 23 Jan. 1925. 839.00/2513.

[69]Russell to Hughes. 26 Jan. 1925. 839.51/2522.

[70]Welles memo of conversation with Velasquez. 26 May 1925. 839.51/2626.

President and was now setting out to destroy the Progresista Party by denying it patronage privileges. Alfonseca would eventually be put forward as a presidential candidate and as such contributed to the revolution of 1930.[71]

Hughes kept pressing for the early ratification of the Convention. He instructed Russell to point out to Vásquez that no new loans could be approved until this had been achieved. Current market conditions, Vásquez was to be told, made it a favorable time for the sale of bonds and the opportunity might be lost to the Dominicans if they delayed too long.[72] Inducements of this kind were in vain, however, as the Dominicans fought their internal political feuds through the spring and summer of 1925. Finally, in August, the Dominican Senate gave conditional approval of the Convention. The condition was that the ratification be accompanied by certain "aclaraciónes," or explanations.

The explanations were four in number. The first explained that the employees of the customs service mentioned in Article one did not include those appointed in accordance with Dominican laws. A second paragraph of the first "aclaración" stipulated that the United States would afford protection to the receivership only when the Dominican government was unable to do so. This was in reference to the provision in Article two of the Convention and was largely a reiteration of the

---

[71] Ibid.

[72] Hughes to Russell. 28 Jan. 1925. 839.51/2516c.

stipulations therein contained. The second explanation provided that none of the bonds of the $25,000,000 loan provided for in the preamble could be issued without the prior consent of the Dominican legislature. The third provided that earlier loans had prior claims on customs receipts. This seems to have been a superfluous amendment since the contract for the bonds of the 1922 issue stated that they had a first lien on customs revenues. The fourth "aclaración" stated that ratifications could not be exchanged until the United States consented to the above clarifying amendments.[73]

The first explanation was identical to the Dominican "aclaraciónes" accompanying the 1907 Convention. At that time they were given cognizance by an exchange of notes between the two governments. They were not treated as having the force of obligations incurred but, rather, as an exchange of views explaining how each party interpreted certain passages in the Convention. The second, third and fourth explanations are insignificant because they altered nothing in the treaty relationship to be established.

Anticipating that the Dominicans would attempt to have certain explanations accepted by the United States, Orme Wilson had prepared a memo concerning them. He concluded that there was no substantial reason not to accept them through an exchange of the type utilized in 1907. He pointed out that only

---

[73]From a copy of the Dominican "aclaraciónes" to the Convention of 1924. Undated. 839.51/2662.

the first had ever become an "annoyance" and for many years Pulliam had managed to administer the customs service without controversy.[74] Wilson, however, had anticipated that all of the "aclaraciónes" would be the same as those submitted in 1907, and he did not anticipate the manner in which they were to be submitted. Two weeks after Wilson had prepared this memo, on August 27, Federico Alvarez, Secretary of the Dominican Legation, presented the clarifying amendments as an integral part of the instrument of ratification. Wilson unhesitatingly informed him that this was unacceptable. The only form in which they might be accepted, he explained, was by an exchange of notes as had been done in 1907. Alvarez replied that he understood this and drafted a telegram to his government requesting an instrument of ratification omitting amendments.[75]

It was not until October 5, however, that such an instrument was forthcoming. In the meantime the United States made it abundantly clear that the explanations would not be acceptable in any form that implied additions to the Convention.[76] In the face of this attitude the Dominican government finally surrendered on the issue. On October 5, 1924, Ariza delivered a note to the Department stipulating that the explanations

---

[74]Wilson memo on Dominican "aclaraciónes." 14 Aug. 1925. 839.51/2658.

[75]Wilson memo of conversation with Alvarez. 27 Aug. 1925. 839.51/2657.

[76]Kellogg to Russell. 10 Sept. 1925. 839.51/2652.

". . . in no wise change the text of the Convention and only serve to dispel any doubt that may arise concerning its interpretation."[77] On the part of the Dominican government the "aclaraciónes" gained expression by being incorporated into the resolution passed by the Dominican Congress approving the Convention. While no longer an integral part of the Convention they did, nevertheless, require a response from the United States.

On October 24, at the time ratifications were exchanged, Frank B. Kellogg, Secretary of State after the departure of Hughes, handed a note to Ariza giving the interpretation of his government to the status of the Dominican explanations. It was stipulated that ratification was of the Convention itself and included none of the amendments appended to it by the resolution of the Dominican Congress. As well as being unnecessary, Kellogg continued, it was impossible for the President of the United States to put into force any provisions except those approved by the United States Senate. As to the explanations themselves, Kellogg wrote that if he understood them correctly they were in entire agreement with the interpretation given to the Convention by the United States. Only with regard to the first explanation did Kellogg elaborate. As understood by his government, Kellogg explained, Article one of the Convention did not exclude the appointment of customs personnel by the

---

[77] For. Rel. II. 1925. Ariza to Kellogg. 5 Oct. 1925. 839.51/2673. p. 53.

Dominican president. These would not, however, be authorized to participate in the collection of revenues or in any other duty or function of the receivership except with the approval of the General Receiver.[78]

The outcome was, then, that the Dominican explanations included in the resolution approving the Convention were treated as an expression of the sense of the Dominican Congress. The United States merely replied that its interpretation of the Convention was in agreement with that given by the Dominican government as expressed in the "aclaraciónes" if it ". . . understood them (the "aclaraciónes") correctly."[79] The Dominican explanations were not a part of the Convention and served only as the basis for discussion in case disputes later arose over those provisions of the Convention to which they were applicable. With ratifications exchanged on October 24, 1925, the treaty was proclaimed in force on October 26.

Throughout the negotiations leading to the conclusion of the revised Customs Convention, two purposes are apparent in United States policy. The first was a desire to assist the Dominicans in bringing order to their financial and political affairs. This can be seen in the agreement to modify Article one to ease the terms of the amortization of the loans. In this instance the United States proved willing to sacrifice

---

[78]*Ibid*. Kellogg to Ariza. 24 Oct. 1925. 839.51/2673. pp. 54-55.

[79]*Ibid*. p. 54.

the added security that had been provided to American purchasers of Dominican bonds contained in that portion of the article pertaining to the remittance to the sinking fund of fifty per cent of the customs collections in excess of $3,000,000. This was reduced to ten per cent of collections in excess of $4,000,000 in the new Convention. "Permanent" financing, which, by itself, had proved insufficient to divert a larger share of customs receipts to the Dominican government, was continued by the Convention. The provision in the Convention for the issuance of bonds up to $25,000,000 was intended to assist the Dominican government to achieve financial stability and to continue a program of internal development that could not have been accomplished by Dominican resources alone.

By far the more significant purpose in American policy was the promotion of its own interests. Even the generosity evidenced in the financial concessions made to the Dominicans was not entirely a selfless act. The United States hoped that financial stability would promote political stability in the Dominican Republic. If this could be achieved it would remove one of the danger spots in the Caribbean that had been a distraction to the United States during World War I. There was, of course, no threat to American security in this area from a non-American power during the 1920's. Only a very shortsighted statesman, however, could have viewed this as a permanent situation.

Even more obvious is the evidence that the financial aid given to the Dominicans was favorable to American economic interests. The bonds of the $25,000,000 loan would be purchased by American investors. Owing to the existence of the receivership, there was little or no risk involved. Payment of the annual interest and amortization was withheld before any revenue derived from customs was remitted to the Dominican government. It cannot be gainsaid, however, that the Dominicans themselves received a fair return from American policy. They were in need of the loans and could not have obtained them without the security to investors provided for in the convention.

United States economic interests were also well protected by the most favored nation agreement. Dominican national pride was appeased to a limited degree by the deletion from the Convention of the provision requiring the consent of the United States before the Dominican government could modify its tariff schedule. The most favored nation agreement prevented the Dominicans from enacting discriminatory tariffs against American imports. At the same time, the Dominican government agreed not to lower tariffs to such an extent that customs collections would be insufficient to meet the debt service.

Hughes, throughout his tenure as Secretary of State, sought to improve United States relations with Latin America. His Dominican policy was designed to promote this end. The most obvious example of this was the termination of the occupation. That this was an important step in the right direction is not to be denied. Hughes, however, may have exaggerated its effects when he remarked that ". . . the significant thing in our interventions was not that we went in but that we came out."[80] Latin Americans, whether fairly or unfairly, were not greatly impressed merely because the United States desisted, in this instance, from a practice which, in its premises, they detested. Particularly were they unimpressed since the United States continued to defend the right to intervene given certain conditions.

Relations with the Dominican Republic in this period are a concrete example of the character of Hughes' attempt to improve the standing of the United States throughout the hemisphere. The United States was in a position to dictate the terms of the new customs convention and to determine whether there was even to be one. The treaty of 1907 provided complete security to American economic and political interests. By negotiating with the Dominican government, by agreeing to ease the terms of the retirement of its bonded indebtedness and by relaxing restrictions on tariff modification in return for a most favored nation agreement, Hughes indicated an inclination on the part of the United States to treat its hemispheric neighbors as equal partners at the bargaining table.

These negotiations were largely of a nominal character. An attempt has been made to show that the two concessions were made at the initiative of the United States. Dominican efforts to gain further concessions were rejected, in some instances peremptorily so. Though there was a good deal more motion than substance in these exchanges, it is of some significance that

---

[80]Hughes. Hemisphere Relations. p. 76.

concessions were made at all. Even so, these too failed to gain the goodwill of Latin America. Hughes' effort went largely unnoticed in an era of bitter and widespread anti-Americanism. A more dramatic policy was needed to allay the suspicions accumulated during three decades. Such a policy would wait for a later administration.

CHAPTER III

INTERLUDE

The Latin American policy of the United States formulated by Hughes was, in the main, adhered to by his successor, Frank Kellogg, during the next four years. The Coolidge administration, after Hughes' departure in 1925, did revert on occasion to the policies of an earlier era. This is apparent chiefly in Nicaraguan affairs where what were regarded as special circumstances dictated a return of the Marines in 1927. At the same time, however, it is fair to point out that it was during the Coolidge years that a rapprochement with Mexico was effected. This required sensitive and conciliatory diplomacy.

Relations between the United States and the Dominican Republic between 1925 and 1929 were by and large uneventful. No circumstance arose to provoke or even to suggest a challenge to the course set by Hughes in the preceding five years. A review of Dominican relations during these years will demonstrate the continuity of policy from Hughes to Stimson. It will also show how the way was prepared for the Dominican political crisis of 1930 that would confront the United States with a set of conditions testing the non-interventionist course pursued since 1924.

Two issues arose after 1925 in Dominican affairs requiring more than the routine attention of the State Department. The first of these concerned the desire of the Dominican government to float a $10,000,000 loan in 1926. This, according to the terms of the Convention of 1924, required the approval of the United States. The second issue arose in connection with the decision by Horacio Vásquez in 1927 to extend his presidential term, due to end in August, 1928, from four to six years. In light of the past involvement by the United States in the domestic affairs of the Republic, and, because of the stake that it had in the continued political stability of that country, the State Department was keenly interested in Vásquez's decision and its potential consequences.

It will be recalled that the general approval by the United States, expressed in the preamble to the Convention of 1924, of a loan or loans amounting to $25,000,000 was not intended as a final statement on the subject. The Convention merely stated that such a loan appeared to be in the best interests of the Dominican Republic. Article three of the Convention required approval by the United States prior to the issuance of bonds for all or any part of the amount stipulated in the preamble or any other increase in the public debt.

It was not until 1926 that the Dominican government requested approval of another loan. The Dominican Minister at Washington, Angel Morales, submitted a proposal for a $10,000,000 bond issue. In his note to the Department he explained that the proceeds were needed for port improvements, highway construction, an aqueduct for Santo Domingo, irrigation projects, construction of school houses, and contributions to a new banking institution for small farmers.[1] All of these except the last fell under the

---

[1]U.S. Dept. of State. Papers Relating to the Foreign Relations of the United States. II. 1926. Washington, D.C. 1941. Morales to Kellogg. 14 Oct. 1926. 839.51/2830. p. 40.

general heading of public works. Most of the projects had been inaugurated by the military government.

The State Department raised no objection to a loan but was inclined to allow the sale of bonds for only $4,000,000 or $5,000,000 immediately. The balance of the $10,000,000 could be sold as the need arose. Evan E. Young, American Minister to the Dominican Republic, urged that permission be granted for the issuance of bonds for the full $10,000,000 at once. He argued that the need was great and that the Dominican Congress and the country at large favored the loan at that time. The Dominican Congress, he pointed out, was subject to sudden shifts in political alignment. It might later block the sale of the balance of the bond issue in order to embarrass President Vásquez.[2]

In further support of his case Young reported that Vásquez, to show his good faith, had suggested that the funds raised by the sale of the bonds be held by the fiscal agent of the loan and turned over to the Dominican government as required to finance the projects for which the loan was being made. With this provision, Young explained, any alteration in the amounts or purposes of the loan would be subject to approval of the department. Under these conditions Young strongly urged approval of the Dominican proposal.[3]

---

[2]*Ibid*. Young to Kellogg. 25 Oct. 1926. 839.51/2834. pp. 41-42.

[3]*Ibid*. p. 41.

Kellogg was not yet convinced. He doubted the ability of the Dominican government to utilize such a large amount of money efficiently. To Young's urgings he replied that the Department regarded the loan of $10,000,000 and the program that had inspired its request as too ambitious and likely to result in "unwise" expenditures.[4] He added, however, that if the Dominican government, in view of the domestic problems facing it, was determined to issue bonds in the amount of $10,000,000 it might be approved if two conditions were met. First, the sum of $3,000,000 would be turned over to the Dominican government for use in 1927. The remaining $7,000,000 was to be deposited in a New York bank to be withdrawn as required. Secondly, to determine when this balance was required, a Public Works Board was to be established. The board would be composed of three members, one to be appointed by the Dominican President, one by the American Minister at Santo Domingo, and one by the General Receiver of Dominican customs. The latter two held their posts at the pleasure of the President of the United States. This, in effect, gave the United States a controlling majority on the suggested Public Works Board. Kellogg was not too explicit concerning the board's functions. He merely stated that it should exercise "some form of control" over the expenditures on the projects for which the loan had been requested.[5]

---

[4]<u>Ibid</u>. Kellogg to Young. 28 Oct. 1926. 839.51/2842a. p. 44.

[5]<u>Ibid</u>. p. 43.

This plan was little short of a modified version of the demand for a financial adviser made in 1915-1916. The major difference, of course, was that the financial adviser was to have controlled all expenditures regardless of the source of the revenue. Had Kellogg's proposal been pressed upon the Dominicans it would have amounted to a sharp departure from the Dominican policy formulated by Hughes. It was not pressed, however. Indeed, it was never presented to the Dominican government.

Young recognized at once the futility of such a proposal. He advised Kellogg that it would be unacceptable to the Dominicans. He offered a plan of his own designed to mollify the Secretary's suspicions concerning Dominican financial sagacity. He proposed that the proceeds of the bond issue of $10,000,000 be turned over to the Dominican government over a three year period. Four million was to be made available in 1927 and a like amount the following year. The balance of $2,000,000 would be turned over during the third year. Nor would each yearly installment be made available in a lump sum but would require the assurance of the Dominican government that it would make withdrawals only as the need arose. In Young's view this was, while not totally safe, much the wiser course.[6]

This proposal, though not as offensive as the Kellogg plan, was still an implicit expression of distrust in Dominican integrity and judgment and would have been galling to them. Aside

---

[6]*Ibid*. Young to Kellogg. 30 Oct. 1926. 839.51/2842. p. 44.

from this it had other objectionable features. It would have required the Dominican government to pay interest on $10,000,000 which they had no assurance of receiving in full for at least three years. It might have been arranged to sell the bonds only as the Dominican government could show, to the satisfaction of the United States, the need. This would have required each time, however, the consent of the Dominican Congress, a procedure that Young had already advised against. Young's plan would have required a continuing review by the State Department of the projects the Dominicans hoped to carry out with the loan. In addition to opening the door to an endless haggling with the Dominican government likely to result in bad feeling on both sides, the plan proposed by Young would have involved the United States more intimately in Dominican domestic affairs than was desirable. It had been the American purpose, since 1920, to disentangle itself as much as possible from this involvement.

Moreover, nothing in the Convention of 1924, by stipulation or even implication, granted to the United States control of the expenditure of funds derived from a loan. That treaty stipulated only that the United States could allow or prevent an increase in the Dominican public debt. If the conviction was that the sums obtained from any loan would be expended unwisely or dishonestly--and the Dominican record in this regard was not such that it encouraged confidence--the State Department could have rejected the request. That, however, was the extent of its treaty rights and responsibilities.

To what extent these considerations influenced the final decision not to impose conditions on the approval of the loan would be difficult to estimate. As finally approved there were no conditions, however. Morales repeated the request of his government for approval of the loan on November 11. In his note to Kellogg the request differed only slightly from the original of less than a month before. It was now proposed that the bonds for the full $10,000,000 be issued in two series of $5,000,000 each, one in 1927 and one the following year.[7] In his reply on November 19, Kellogg approved the loan in the manner proposed. The only stipulation required by the United States was that it was to be understood that these bonds and any bonds issued in the future would be secured by the customs receipts. The life of the 1924 Convention would be extended until all bonds were fully redeemed.[8]

Perhaps the most accurate explanation for Kellogg's about face from suggesting, though not actually proposing, a Public Works Board for controlling to some extent the expenditures made possible by the loan, to unconditionally approving it rests in the fact that outside of the Department his original position found little support. On November 8, Young confirmed Kellogg's view that bankers, businessmen and the General Receiver were unanimously agreed that, except for stipulations as to amounts

---

[7]Ibid. Morales to Kellogg. 11 Nov. 1926. 839.51/2857. pp. 45-46.

[8]Ibid. Kellogg to Morales. 19 Nov. 1926. 839.51/2858. p. 49.

and purposes, the loan should be approved unconditionally. For his part, Young saw ". . . no reason to modify in any particular . . ." the suggestions he had made previously.[9]

The end result of this relatively minor affair in United States-Dominican relations was that the Dominicans obtained essentially what they desired without having to accept offensive conditions in return. That no such conditions were imposed or ever made the import of a formal proposal to the Dominican government is, in the final analysis, the most important point to be made relative to this incident. It is significant, however, that State Department officers were still thinking in terms of the type of control suggested by Kellogg and Young. Their views are indicative of a certain ambivalence in the formulation of Caribbean policy. It was, to a degree, a reversion to that patronizing attitude of an earlier period when the United States had deputed to itself the right to oversee the efficient and honest administration of Dominican domestic affairs. This was precisely what Hughes had tried to avoid. Hughes had committed the United States to a policy of treating the Caribbean nations with a proper respect for their status as independent nations. In the end this approach won out. It is of some importance, however, that it was not yet established policy.

It would be misleading to make any general statement on the nature of the Caribbean, or even the Dominican, policy of

---

[9] _Ibid._ Young to Kellogg. 8 Nov. 1926. 839.51/2842. p. 44.

the United States during the Coolidge years drawn from this example alone. In the only other significant issue it had to deal with during this period, the prolongation by Vásquez of his presidential term in 1927 and his decision to stand for reelection in 1930, the United States maintained a perfectly correct attitude. It will be shown that at the outset of these events the State Department established a policy of non-interference and upheld it throughout.

One might, of course, inquire as to the significance of this. It may be asked why it should have been expected that the posture assumed by the American government might have been otherwise. The policy pursued was, after all, nothing more nor less than what one sovereign nation expects of another. In reply it need only be recalled that the United States had a special relationship with the Dominican Republic established by treaty, and in the recent past the United States had intervened on a large scale in Dominican domestic affairs. Moreover, American economic interests had invested heavily in Dominican bonds and the United States government had pledged to secure their redemption. Should Vásquez's evasion of the Dominican constitution have resulted in political chaos threatening the security of the customs receivership, the United States would have been faced with an unwanted problem. The State Department was aware of this possibility. While it declined to interfere in any way with the political maneuvering that might bring on such a situation, it never committed itself to non-interference in the event that it actually came about. For a better understanding of this affair a brief discussion of the Dominican political background is in order.

Horacio Vásquez had been a popular and influential political figure in the Dominican Republic since the assassination of Ulises Heureaux in 1899. He could have had the presidency in 1907 but declined to put himself forward because his cousin and close political associate, Rámon Cáceres, sought the office. To oppose Cáceres would have caused a split in the Horacista party and continuation of the turmoil of the preceding eight years. Recognizing that his country needed peace above all, he stepped out of the political picture entirely contrary to the urgings of his many partisans.[10] Throughout his political career, Vásquez had shown a degree of selfless patriotism uncommon among Dominican politicians. In 1928, Evan E. Young wrote that Vásquez was able, honest and sincerely interested in advancing the welfare of his country.[11] But Young was not so sanguine that he saw only Vásquez's virtues. He balanced his positive assessment by pointing out that Vásquez also loved the political game and enjoyed the powers of his office and was not prepared to surrender them.[12] The Constitution of 1924, however, prohibited him from serving consecutive terms. At first Vásquez hoped to continue his control of the national government through

---

[10]Sumner Welles. Naboth's Vineyard. II. (New York, 1928). p. 639.

[11]Young to Kellogg. 26 Oct. 1928. 728.3915/369.

[12]Ibid.

his political party, the Partido Nacional. In order to accomplish this he had to be certain of the loyalty of his successor. For this role Vásquez had selected José Dolores de Alfonseca, his principal adviser since 1924. In this capacity Alfonseca had attained a large degree of control over the distribution of patronage. As seen in the preceding chapter, his use of this power had incurred the wrath of Vice-President Velásquez who felt that members of his Progresista Party had not received their fair share of offices. Velásquez also accused Alfonseca of undermining his influence with Vásquez.

Alfonseca had made other enemies as well. Young had reported as early as 1926 that Alfonseca was not a popular figure in the Republic. Young felt that Vásquez had erred in putting Alfonseca forward so early as a candidate for the presidency. Other presidential hopefuls, Velásquez in particular, would see, or pretend to see, in every government move an effort to promote Alfonseca's interests. It also had provided a candidate against whom the opposition could unite.[13]

A campaign of vilification of Alfonseca continued throughout 1926 and 1927. With the elections of 1928 less than a year away, Vásquez found himself with a candidate whose election--which, of course, could be assured--would have provoked the kind of unrest that had existed in 1916. In the Latin American political milieu electoral frauds were and, to a lesser extent,

---

[13]Young to Kellogg. 6 Apr. 1926. 839.00/2949.

still are an acceptable if not honored political practice. If, however, one so elected is not popular to begin with, or is unwilling or unable to impose a harsh rule, he is likely to enjoy only a brief tenure in office. This was the case with Alfonseca.

Illustrative of this truism is the fact that Vásquez was able to remain in office for two years after his scheduled departure by what can only be called an extravagantly loose interpretation of the Dominican constitution. As Alfonseca was decidedly not acceptable as a successor, Vásquez had, by April, 1927, determined that his party could maintain control of the government only by his continuing as president of the Republic. The provision of the Constitution of 1924 prohibiting re-election proved not to be an insurmountable obstacle. Vásquez circumvented it with the expedient rationalization that he had not been elected under that instrument. The Constitution of 1924, he argued, had not taken effect until the withdrawal of the American occupation forces. This occurred simultaneously with his inauguration in August, 1924. He had been elected in the preceding March. He contended that he had been elected under the Constitution of 1908 which provided for a six year presidential term. His term did not end, therefore, until 1930.[14] The Dominican Congress, controlled by Horacistas, enacted a law approving the extension

---

[14]For. Rel. II. 1927. Young to Kellogg. 12 Apr. 1927. 839.00/3049. p. 549.

of Vásquez's term on May 2, 1927.[15]

Leaving aside the futility of such an exercise, it is unnecessary to determine the merit of Vásquez's interpretation of the Dominican constitution. It is sufficient to point out the suprising fact that the novelty of his situation was not even suspected until 1927, after he had been in office for three years.

The reaction to this maneuver by the State Department was mild. Young first heard rumors about the project in February, 1927. He advised that if any representations protesting the action were to be made that they be of a very informal nature. In his view the United States should not commit itself to any position difficult to maintain.[16] In its reply to Young's dispatch the Department concurred fully in this approach.[17]

A few days later, on March 8, Young was granted an interview with Vásquez. The Dominican president explained that he had not yet made a final decision on the prolongation of his term. He admitted to Young that many members of his own party supported the measure for purely selfish reasons. So long as he, Vásquez, remained in office their political appointments were secure. For his part, Vásquez told Young, the only reason for giving serious consideration to the project was his desire

---

[15]Ibid. Young to Kellogg. 2 May 1927. 839.00/3053. p. 551.

[16]Ibid. Young to Kellogg. 28 Feb. 1927. 839.00/3053. p. 545.

[17]Ibid. Joseph C. Grew (Acting Sec.) to Young. 3 Mar. 1927. p. 546.

to promote the continuation of the progress his country had experienced during the preceding three years.[18]

Young, at this point, apparently believed that Vásquez really did not favor the extension of his term from four to six years. His support of the project was in response to the pressure of his friends and supporters. Young regarded the prolongation as a certainty, however, despite Vásquez's disclaimers that he had not reached a final decision. The only means by which the project could be defeated, he reported, were through strong, formal protests from the United States. He reiterated his opposition to this approach. He pointed out that should anything of this nature be done, the United States would be held responsible for any evils that befell the Dominican Republic under a new administration. Young advised only friendly counsel discouraging the project.[19]

As the measure providing for the extension of Vásquez's term neared a vote in the Dominican legislature, with approval a certainty, Young advised going an oblique step further. He suggested that Angel Morales, the Dominican Minister at Washington, be called in and told informally that the responsibility for any instability created in the Dominican Republic by the prolongation of Vásquez'a term rested squarely upon the Dominicans themselves.[20]

---

[18]*Ibid*. Young to Kellogg. 8 Mar. 1927. 839.00/3038. p. 546.

[19]*Ibid*. p. 546.

[20]*Ibid*. Young to Kellogg. 31 Mar. 1927. 839.00/3045. p. 547.

Young's suggestion might have accomplished two things. First, it was a means of indicating disapproval by the Department without saying so directly. Secondly, if, as some Dominicans predicted, the extension of Vásquez's term resulted in armed outbreaks the United States could show that it had not been a party to the maneuver.

The Department, however, would have no part of Young's suggestion. Kellogg replied that he saw no reason to hope or believe that it would have a favorable effect. Morales was too strongly in favor of the measure. Over and above that, he wrote, the matter was strictly a Dominican domestic affair and should be left to the Dominicans to settle as they might desire. Young, however, was granted permission to make his informal representations in Santo Domingo.[21]

While the Department maintained this attitude of complete aloofness, Young went about the business of determining just what the consequences of the Vásquez measure might be. He approached Vásquez about the dangers of political unrest and, perhaps, armed disturbances if he remained in office beyond 1928. Vásquez replied that he foresaw no such result.[22]

Young, by this time disabused of any notions he may have once held concerning the purity of Vásquez's motives, was aware

---

[21]*Ibid*. Kellogg to Young. 2 Apr. 1927. 839.00/3045 pp. 547-548.

[22]*Ibid*. Young to Kellogg. Report of interview with Vasquez. 12 Apr. 1927. 839.00/3049. p. 549.

that the Dominican president had every reason to be biased in the matter. To obtain a more objective evaluation he sought the views of Francisco Peynado whom Young portrayed as representative of the best Dominican opinion. Peynado felt that Vásquez had done a superlative job during the preceding three years. He was opposed nevertheless, to the extension of his term. He was opposed as well to any effort by the United States to prevent it. Young reassured him on this point. Peynado then expressed the view, claimed by him to be held by many, that while he was opposed to the prolongation of Vásquez's term he preferred this to the election of Alfonseca. The latter, he said, would certainly be elected if Vásquez decided to retire in 1928. Alfonseca would be unable to control his own party after being elected. Furthermore, he would be totally lacking in support from the various interest and power groups influential in Dominican politics. The result would be disorder and eventual breakdown of domestic peace. The extension of Vásquez's term was objectionable from many standpoints, but it was the lesser of the two evils. Peynado did not believe that any disturbances would occur if Vásquez remained in office beyond 1928.[23]

Vice-President Velásquez saw things in a different light. He told Young that it was certain that disturbances protesting the extension of the Vásquez term would occur. He believed that outbreaks would commence in August, 1928, when Vásquez

---

[23]*Ibid*. Report of Interview with Peynado. p. 550.

had been scheduled to leave office. Velásquez urged that the United States take whatever steps necessary to cause the project to be abandoned. It was his intention, he stated, to proceed to Washington to press this view upon the State Department. Young discouraged this notion informing him that it would serve no useful purpose and that the United States had no intention of interfering in the matter unless its outcome resulted in threats to American lives and property.[24] Here for the first time it was intimated that, while the United States would refrain from interfering in a purely Dominican domestic issue, it upheld its right to take action where its own interests were affected by the outcome.

It was hinted at again when Velásquez, heedless of Young's discouragements, visited Washington during the following August. He was received there by Stokely W. Morgan, Chief of the Latin American Affairs Division of the State Department. Velásquez began by protesting the extension of Vásquez's term as illegal and not in accord with the Evacuation Convention of 1924. He wanted to know why the United States had not vigorously protested the action. Morgan patiently explained that his government regarded it as purely a Dominican concern. It did not feel justified in interfering in any way whatsoever. Morgan then pointed out that Velásquez, and others who felt as he did, would have been the first to object had the United States done

---

[24] _Ibid_. Report of interview with Velásquez. pp. 549-550.

anything of the kind suggested by the former Dominican vice-president.[25]

Velásquez congratulated Morgan on the "highly laudable" stance taken by the United States. He went on to inquire what the attitude of the United States would be should a revolution--which he predicted--break out to prevent Vásquez from serving out the added two years of his term. He stated that,

> . . . the Department should not by abstaining from action permit the rights of the people to be infringed, and then by forceful intervention prevent the people from asserting their rights.[26]

Morgan replied that the United States would regret to see the outbreak of political disturbances, especially since there seemed to be no just grounds for them. The prolongation of Vásquez's term, he argued, had been approved by the Dominican people through their representatives in Congress. Morgan was not being naive. Velásquez had pretended to be more interested in the preservation of the rights of the Dominican people than he was in being their president. Morgan replied in kind. He pretended to believe that the opinions of the people swayed the Dominican legislators. He did not evade the question put to him by Velásquez, however. He replied that what attitude the United States would assume in case of disorders would have to await developments and would depend upon the circumstances

---

[25] Ibid. Morgan memo of conversation with Velasquez. 27 Aug. 1927. 839.00/3091. p. 553.

[26] Ibid. p. 554.

prevailing at the time.[27]

While Morgan's observation certainly did not comprise a threat neither did it commit the United States to inaction regardless of developments resulting from the extension of Vásquez's term. Taken together with Young's comment on the subject it is a clear indication that the United States did not intend to keep its hands entirely off Dominican affairs should they present a danger to American interests. So long as Dominican domestic issues did not adversely affect these interests the Dominicans would be left to resolve them without interference from Washington. In this way the responsibility for meeting its obligations was left to the Dominicans. Only when failure to fulfill this responsibility had been made evident would the United States consider countermeasures.

Based on the information available to it, the State Department concluded that there was little danger that the extension of Vásquez's presidential term would result in disturbances endangering American economic or political interests. Quite the contrary was true. It appeared that unrest would occur unless Vásquez remained in office. This solution then appeared to be in the best interests of the United States. This is not, however, sufficient evidence for believing that the State Department refrained from opposing the manipulations of the Dominican constitution because it favored the prolongation of the Vásquez term. Vásquez could not remain in office indefinitely. Sooner

---

[27]*Ibid.* p. 554.

or later someone with less prestige and popularity would have to be elected to the presidency. The stability of Dominican institutions would ultimately have to be tested. As long as political stability depended upon a personality it could only be considered temporary. The internal evidence also refutes the notion that the United States favored the extension of the Vásquez term. It has been shown that, while no formal representations were made protesting the measure, it was discouraged through the friendly counsel of the American Minister.

The position adopted by the United States respecting the extension of Vásquez's presidential term would be maintained during the crisis that developed in 1930 when Vásquez decided to stand for re-election. The Dominican Constitution of 1908, under which Vásquez claimed to have been elected to a six year term, permitted the president to succeed himself. According to that instrument, therefore, Vásquez could have sought re-election in 1930, although for only a four year term in accordance with the Constitution of 1924. To mollify his critics, however, Vásquez had caused the act of the Dominican Congress extending his first term to include an article forbidding him to stand for re-election in 1930.[28] This, of course, could be and would be changed without much difficulty.

Throughout the summer of 1928, Young forwarded information to the Department indicating that Vásquez intended to stand for

---

[28]*Ibid.* Morgan memo on Dominican situation. 839.00/3053. p. 553.

re-election in 1930.[29] On October 17, in an interview with Vásquez, Young counselled against his seeking another term. He told the Dominican president that he regarded him as the outstanding figure in the country. No other prospective candidate could wield his influence and authority. Young urged him, however, to consider very carefully the consequences of his re-nomination to the future political development of his country. Vásquez replied that he had not made a final decision whether to again be a candidate in 1930. He added that he was disinclined to accept his party's renomination. Of this disclaimer Young wrote that, ". . . while it may well have been intended as a frank and sincere expression of his present attitude, it should be accepted with some reserve."[30] Indeed, for Vásquez had made similar remarks relative to the extension of his presidential term in 1927.

The Department did consider making stronger representations to Vásquez. In July Young had reported that Vásquez would probably endorse Alfonseca as the candidate for the National Party. At the same time he would leave the door open for his own renomination and re-election.[31] Upon reading this report Orme Wilson of the Latin American Affairs Division suggested that, owing to the unpopularity of Alfonseca and the probable outbreak of disturbances in the event of his candidacy, Vásquez

---

[29]See specifically dispatches 839.00/3150, 58, 60, 66, 67, and 70, sent from Santo Domingo from July through September, 1928.

[30]Young to Kellogg. 17 Oct. 1928. 839.00/3172.

[31]Young to Kellogg. 2 Jul. 1928. 839.00/3138.

be influenced to endorse someone else. Such an attempt to influence Vásquez, he continued,

> . . . would amount technically to unjustifiable interference in the internal affairs of the Republic - on the other hand, if Mr. Young thinks that there is a possibility of accomplishing anything, the end would justify the means.[32]

In a marginal note, Francis White, Assistant Secretary of State, replied that he wished to talk with Young before commenting on Wilson's suggestion.[33] Young visited Washington later in the summer. The outcome of his conversations with White and other officials of the Department are revealed in his dispatch from Santo Domingo of October 26. After stating his general assessment of the Dominican political scene he wrote,

> It is the opinion of the Legation, and an opinion which it feels certain is shared by the Department, that the question of re-election is one concerning which no formal or official move should be made on our part to influence or affect the final outcome.[34]

He went on to say that such informal representations as he had made had been presented as his own views and not those of his government. Young believed that this was the correct approach and pointed to its results as proof. He believed that there had been a vast improvement in United States-Dominican relations and an improved attitude on the part of Dominicans toward the United States. This, he wrote, was the result of the

---

[32]Wilson memo to Francis White, Assistant Secretary. 13 Jul. 1928. 839.00/3139.

[33]Marginal note by White attached to Wilson memo cited in footnote above.

[34]Young to Kellogg. 26 Oct. 1928. 738.3915/369.

accumulated evidence that it had scrupulously refrained from interfering in Dominican domestic affairs while at the same time evincing an earnest desire to afford it every appropriate assistance.[35]

Young was not unaware of the possible future consequences of Vásquez's decision to continue his dominance of Dominican politics. Vásquez, in Young's view, was without doubt the ablest political leader in the Republic. This, combined with his honesty and patriotism, made him a rarity among Latin American politicians of the day. In this respect, Young continued, there was much to be said in favor of his re-election. He then observed that,

> On the other hand, if the day ever comes when political life . . . is established on a firm foundation, that foundation will have been constructed from a general respect for, and obedience to the Constitution and the laws of the land. The longer these countries indulge in the pastime of amending the Constitution to effect the maintenance of power . . . so much the longer will it be before their political life is established on a firm and sound basis.[36]

Two points are clear from Young's dispatch. First, the United States foresaw that future difficulties were likely in the Dominican Republic so long as stability there depended on the influence of a single individual. It was quite apparent that disturbances were even more likely as a result of Vásquez's attempt to maintain his influence by the manipulation of the institutions of government. If one of their

---

[35] *Ibid.*

[36] *Ibid.*

most highly esteemed citizens held little regard for constitutional procedures, what importance must lesser citizens have placed in them. Secondly, the United States clearly intended to do nothing in an official way to prevent Vásquez from being re-elected.

On November 21, 1928, the obstacles in the way of Vásquez's succeeding himself in 1930 were removed. Not only was that part of the 1927 law extending his first term but forbidding his re-election repealed, but for good measure, Article forty-four of the Constitution of 1924 prohibiting re-election was removed as well. At the procedure Young observed that, ". . . there can now be little question of his intention to accept another term."[37]

The attempt to realize this intention was destined to result in precisely the kind of disturbances that had been foreseen. In part at least, Vásquez's efforts to be re-elected in 1930 provoked the revolution of that year. In light of this, the extension by Vásquez of his term and his decision to stand for re-election held a significance beyond reflecting the general nature of the Dominican policy of the United States. The revolution of 1930 that brought Rafael Leonidas Trujillo to power would test severely the policy of non-interference maintained since 1924.

---

[37]Young to Kellogg. 21 Nov. 1928. 839.00/3182.

CHAPTER IV

THE EMERGENCE OF TRUJILLO

The manipulation of the Dominican constitution by Vásquez brought on the revolution foreseen by Young and other observers. The unstable political atmosphere generated by the ouster of Vásquez provided Raphael Leonidas Trujillo with an opportunity to gain the ascendance in Dominican politics. Trujillo proved to be equal to the situation. He was elected to the presidency through fraud and intimidation in 1930 and thereafter established a ruthless dictatorship that did not end until his assassination in 1961. The response by the Hoover administration to the revolution, fraudulent election and the financial crisis resulting from the international depression and aggravated by the greed and financial chicanery of the Trujillo dictatorship, illustrates as well as any set of curcumstances in the hemisphere the overall American approach to Latin America in this period.

It has been claimed for Hoover that he inaugurated the Good Neighbor Policy--even to the extent of using the term--and that Franklin Roosevelt merely "adopted and expanded" it.[1] It is true that Hoover made a conscious effort to improve the relations of the United States with the other American republics. That to increase trade may have been the chief motive does not lend

---

[1]DeConde. Hoover's Latin American Policy. p. 124-127. [Respecting the use of the term "good neighbor," DeConde concedes that it had been in use since the time of Henry Clay and that it had a broader application that just the Western Hemisphere.]

a sinister air to the effort.[2] While it is not intended to minimize Hoover's achievements, it will be argued that major differences existed between the reserved nature, the style and, significantly, the results of his hemispheric policy and that of his immediate successor.

In the main, Hoover's Latin American policy adhered to the course plotted by Charles Evans Hughes earlier in the decade. There was a difference in emphasis, however. Hoover was more earnest in his attempts to promote a positive image of the United States. Illustrative of this was his visit to eleven Latin American countries as president-elect in the fall of 1928. By the late twentieth century, Americans have grown accustomed to presidential forays abroad. Taken as a whole, the results of these have been so mixed that an accurate accounting could as easily show a loss as a profit. Compared to the journeys of later presidents, Hoover's was relatively successful. Evenso, too much has been claimed for it.[3] Discerning observers were quick to point out that standing alone the trip would accomplish little in the way of increasing goodwill. C.H. Abbott, an American journalist with ten years experience in Latin America and friendly in his attitude toward Hoover, reported that the

---

[2]William Appleman Williams. "Latin America: Laboratory of American Foreign Policy in the Nineteen-Twenties." Inter-American Economic Affairs. XI. (Autumn, 1957) pp. 3-30. See also: Gardner. Economic Aspects of New Deal Diplomacy. pp. 35-52.

[3]DeConde. Hoover's Latin American Policy. p. 48. See also: Ferrell. Depression Diplomacy. p. 217; and William Starr Myers. The Foreign Policies of Herbert Hoover. (New York and London, 1940) p. 41.

> . . . journey and the contacts then formed will not be sufficient . . . to materially reduce criticism should intervention become necessary. On the other hand, should intervention be avoided and conditions be relieved through other means, the effect of the Hoover trip would be very much more beneficial.[4]

Raymond Buell, Director of the Foreign Policy Association, came to the same conclusion. Shortly after Hoover's return to the United States, Buell wrote of the Trip that it could provide the basis for a new understanding between the American states. "But," he continued, "if a new understanding is to be permanently realized, it must be based upon a re-orientation of our Latin American policy."[5] The re-orientation Buell had in mind was one leading away from intervention. The grounds for American intervention were the repeatedly expressed fears that a European government might threaten American security interests by meddling in the domestic instability of a Central American or Caribbean state. These fears, Buell wrote, were unfounded. If such a thing ever did occur, remedial action could be taken ". . . but until [then] . . . I cannot see any possible justification of an intervention policy whose chief end is to forestall a possible, if not wholly imaginary, interference from Europe later on."[6] It is fairly clear that the success of Hoover's trip, however much it may have dramatized his concern for Latin American goodwill,

---

[4]Herbert Hoover Papers: Foreign Affairs: File Box 1018: Letter C.H. Abbott to Warren Graham of Graham Engineering Company who forwarded it to the White House.

[5]Raymond L. Buell. "A New Latin-American Policy." <u>Forum</u>. Vol. 81. (1928) p. 113.

[6]<u>Ibid</u>. p. 116.

could be measured only by his actions after he became president and policy maker.

The key to allaying the suspicion in which the United States was held by its hemispheric neighbors and to defuse the resentment generated by three decades of interventionist practices was a disavowel of that practice for the future.[7] In his memoirs, Hoover claims to have avowed a non-interventionist policy.[8] Yet, there is nothing in the public record to support this claim. The record that does exist does not serve Hoover particularly well. On April 13, 1929, in an address before the Gridiron Club of Washington, D.C., Hoover was as explicit in his stance on intervention as he ever would be. In this statement he deplored a "sinister notion" that had gained an unwarranted currency relative to the policies of the United States toward the smaller nations of Latin America. That notion was ". . . fear of an era of the mistakenly called dollar diplomacy." Hoover added:

> The implications that have been colored by that expression are not a part of my conception of international relations. I can say at once that it never has been and ought not to be the policy of the United States to intervene by force to secure or maintain contracts between our citizens and foreign states or their citizens.[9]

---

[7]Raymond L. Buell. "Changes in Our Latin American Policy." The Annals of the American Academy of Political and Social Sciences. Vol. 156. (1931) pp. 126-132. See Also:___. "The Intervention Policy of the United States." Annals: AAAPSS Vol. 138. (1928) p. 72.

[8]Herbert Hoover. Memoirs: the Cabinet and the Presidency. (New York, 1952) p. 334.

[9]William Starr Meyers (compiler and editor). The State Papers and other Public Writings of Herbert Hoover. I. (New York, 1932) p. 30. [Hoover's Memoirs include this passage from the speech minus the phrase ". . . never has been . . ." II. p. 333.]

Hoover went on to say that this attitude not only assured the United States of the confidence of foreign countries but ". . . it is the true expression of the moral rectitude of the United States."[10]

Latin American observers were no doubt pleased to learn that Hoover was repelled by the policy known as "dollar diplomacy" and all of its implications. It was not to be expected, however, that much credit would be placed in this profession when he denied in the same breath that such a policy had ever existed. Nor could they have been much impressed by the proposition that Hoover's assertion was proof of the "moral rectitude" of the United States.

In fairness to Hoover, it should be pointed out that he was unable to give as full attention to Latin America as apparently he had intended. As the depression began to take its social and economic toll, the White House provided supervision of but no initiative in hemispheric relations. Presidential energy, great as it was, was sapped by a host of problems having higher priority. In consequence, the conduct of Latin American affairs became the business of the State Department and its Secretary, Henry L. Stimson. If anything new in the way of a Latin American policy was formulated in these years, it emanated from the Department of State and not from the White House.

One way of discovering the thinking on Latin America that guided policy makers in the State Department is to examine the memorandum on the Monroe Doctrine writtin in 1928 by J. Reuben

---

[10]Ibid. p. 31.

Clark, Undersecretary of State until 1929. Many of the accounts crediting Hoover with initiating the Good Neighbor Policy feature the Clark memorandum as the chief instrument by which the United States removed the cause of Latin American grievances with American interventionist policy.[11] Robert Ferrell calls the Clark memorandum ". . . one of the most important statements of United States policy toward Latin America in the twentieth century. . . ."[12] Hoover himself counts the "publicizing" of the document as one of the measures by which he created goodwill for the United States in the hemisphere.[13]

Notwithstanding these claims, the Clark memorandum was far too limited in scope and purpose to accomplish any such thing and it was hardly new. In the preface to the study, Clark disclaimed any intention to make a definitive statement on the Monroe Doctrine, to say nothing of the larger matter of Latin American policy. The memorandum was, in Clark's words ". . . merely [the] personal expressions of the writer."[14]

Even as a personal expression, Clark did not renounce intervention. He did assert, however, that intervention could not be justified by the Monroe Doctrine. He wrote that ". . . in its

---

[11]De Conde. Hoover's Latin American Policy. pp. 48-50. [See also: Whitaker. Western Hemisphere Idea. p. 135; Ferrell. Depression Diplomacy. p. 221.

[12]Ferrell. Depression Diplomacy. p. 221.

[13]Hoover. Memiors. II. p. 334.

[14]United States Department of State. Memorandum on the Monroe Doctrine. Prepared by J. Reuban Clark. (Washington, D.C., 1930) p. IX.

intervention . . ." the United States might ". . . speak of the right of self-preservation and not of the Monroe Doctrine. . . ." The latter, he continued,

> . . . is not an equivalent for 'self-preservation', and therefore the Monroe Doctrine need not, indeed should not, be invoked in order to cover situations challenging our self-preservation but not within the terms defined by Monroe's declaration. These other situations may be handled, and more wisely so, as matters affecting the national security . . . of the United States . . . ."[15]

In Clark's view, then, intervention could be justified on grounds of national security. This was precisely the view expressed by Charles Evans Hughes in 1923. As such, the Clark memorandum had the same advantages and suffered the same handicaps as had Hughes' too facile distinction. Edward S. Corwin's rebuke of the Hughes statement in 1923 is applicable to the Clark memorandum: ". . . as the Scotchman complained of the claret, the statement gets us 'no forrarder'."[16]

Significantly, the Clark memorandum, with all its limitations, was never advanced as an official policy statement by the United States, although such a step was favored by Stimson but rejected by Hoover.[17] When released, the practical effect of the memorandum amounted to the "personal expressions" of a former Undersecretary of State issued as a public document and not having the force

---

[15] Ibid. p. XXI.

[16] Edward S. Corwin. "The Monroe Doctrine." North American Review. Vol. 218. (1923) p. 721.

[17] Henry Lewis Stimson. Diaries. XV. p. 81. (Microfilm edition, Reel 3) Feb. 9, 1931. Manuscripts and Archives, Yale University Library, New Haven Conn.

of an avowed national policy.

Henry Stimson found a way of getting the view contained in the Clark memorandum before the public wrapped in an official cloak. On February 6, 1931, in an address on Latin American affairs delivered to the Council on Foreign Relations, Stimson reiterated that the Monroe Doctrine was not ". . . an assertion of suzerainty over our sister republics . . . [It] was a declaration of the United States versus Europe--not of the United States versus Latin America."[18] The general policy of the United States in the hemisphere had been a "noble one," Stimson said, aimed at fortifying the independence of its sister republics. He conceded that there were "dark spots" in the record. These, he explained, were the result of a "geographical fact." In the one area vital to the national security of the United States, the Caribbean republics adjacent to or lying in the approaches to the Panama Canal, progress toward stable and responsible government had been slow. "In these locales," he continued, ". . . the violation of the rights of life and property accorded by international law to foreigners . . ." had been endemic, leading to ". . . ripples in the steady current . . ." of United States policy.[19]

Stimson was pleased with the address and viewed it as the enunciation of a "new policy" for Latin America.[20] But its meagre

---

[18]Henry L. Stimson Papers. Speeches, Writing, Statements, Series III. Box 180. Folder 124. Manuscripts and Archives, Yale University Library. New Haven, Conn.

[19]*Ibid*. p. 2.

[20]Stimson. *Diaries*. XVI. pp. 77-78. (Microfilm edition, Reel 3) Feb. 6, 1931.

results hardly warranted that billing, and critics were not slow to point this out. In a lucid appraisal of Stimson's speech, Norman Davis argued that ". . . during the two years . . . since Mr. Hoover took office there has been no positive improvement in our relations with Latin America. Indeed, it is fair to say that the resentment . . . has been greatly intensified. . . ."[21] Davis pointed out that Stimson did not address the "more important questions" affecting United States - Latin American relations.[22] The important question was intervention and this practice was not to be dismissed as a "ripple." Intervention in a Caribbean or Central American state was as deeply felt in Brazil or Argentina as in the smaller countries directly affected. Security interests, Davis conceded, would always be understandable if not just grounds for intervention. But American interventions in Latin America had not been warranted by threats to the nation's security, and Latin Americans had been alarmed by the frequency of intervention and ". . . their animosity has been raised to a fever pitch. . . ."[23]

Sumner Welles, in a broad assessment of the Hoover administration's Latin American policy, concurs with the general conclusions reached by Davis. Welles freely grants that Hoover's intensions were admirable. Moreover, Hoover recognized the implications for United States security that a lack of Latin American good will

---

[21]Norman Davis. "Wanted: A Consistent Latin American Policy." Foreign Affairs. IX. (1933) p. 394.

[22]*Ibid*. p. 549.

[23]*Ibid*. p. 563.

held. His goal was to obtain that good will. But if results are used as the measure of his success, his efforts bore little fruit.[24]

These considerations respecting the general approach of the Hoover administration to Latin America have attempted to show that, however good the intentions, there was no willingness to go the necessary step of renouncing the right of intervention. With respect to that subject, Hoover and Stimson were defensive about past American policy and non-commital about the future. In a final assessment of the foreign policies of the Hoover presidency, Stimson claims much for its Latin American policy. But notably absent is any claim to having established the principle of non-intervention.[25] An examination of relations with the Dominican Republic during the last two and one-half years of Hoover's presidency will show why he did not do so.

In 1928, at the time that Vásquez had decided to put himself forward as a candidate in the election scheduled for 1930, Young had only forecast the possibility of revolution. As 1929 was drawing to a close, the evidence that it was a certainty mounted. As early as October 6, Young had warned that it was unlikely that the country would pass through the elections, scheduled for May 15, 1930, without serious armed uprisings.[26]

---

[24]Sumner Welles. The Time for Decision. (New York and London, 1944) pp. 191-192.

[25]Henry L. Stimson. "Bases of American Foreign Policy during the Past Four Years." Foreign Affairs. XI. (1933) p. 394.

[26]Young to Stimson. 6 Oc. 1929. 839.00/3219.

Earlier Young had explained that the alternatives to revolution as a means of unseating Vásquez were practically non-existent. In the first place the opposition parties were quarreling among themselves and had so far been unable to unite behind one candidate. Young believed that if a coalition could be effected it would make a close race in a fair election.[27] By October, however, no such coalition was in sight. The only serious effort that had met with any success had already disintegrated. Velásquez's progresista Parta and the Liberal Party led by Desiderio Arias[28] had for a brief time combined their efforts. Velásquez had been nominated for the presidency and Juan B. Perez, a Liberal, for the second place on the ticket. Perez, however, declined this empty gesture and the coalition, shaky to begin with, collapsed. Young reported that as a result the various opposition groups were as divided as ever.[29]

Even assuming that a working coalition would be arranged, Young's other condition for a peaceful settlement of the growing Dominican crisis, fair elections, was out of the question. There is ample evidence to show that Vásquez had no intention of losing the contest. As early as the summer of 1929 Vásquez had begun to suppress some of his political opponents. Rafael Estrella Urena, destined to be instrumental in the rise of Trujillo, had organized

---

[27]Young to Stimson. 23 Aug. 1929. 839.00/3208.

[28]The same Arias who had been a prime source of mischief in 1916.

[29]Young to Stimson. Oct. 839.00/3219.

a personalist organization, the so-called Republican Party, to promote his own candidacy for the presidency. Vásquez ordered the army to disrupt a rally being held for Estrella Urena's benefit. For reasons that will later become apparent, the army, of which Trujillo was the commander, did not carry out the full purport of its instructions.[30]

The fact that Vásquez ordered it did indicate, nevertheless, that he was resorting to methods of control for which he had hitherto shown disdain. Young did not believe that his high-handed conduct in this episode was a prelude to dictatorship. He explained that Vásquez's health was deteriorating.

> . . . and his slowly failing powers spur him on to choose the easier course and slowly to abandon the Bismarkian tactics which he has hitherto followed with such great success.[31]

Another indication that the election would be corrupt can be seen in the manipulation of the Dominican electoral law. During the negotiations in 1922 leading to the withdrawal of American Marines a Central Electoral Board had been set up to assure free and fair elections. The Board was empowered to sit in judgment on disputed elections. This had worked out well in the election of 1924. The members of the Board on that occasion had been selected by the common accord of all interested parties. It had a built in flaw, however. Members of the Board were appointed to four year terms. When the terms of the original members expired,

---

[30] Young to Stimson. 20 Jul. 1929. 839.00/3200.

[31] *Ibid.*

replacements were appointed by the Vásquez government. It was in the nature of things that these appointees would be favorable to the Horacistas.

The opposition parties had hoped that there would be reform in the appointments to the Electoral Board before the elections of 1930. Recognizing that this had become a focal point for agitation, Vásquez attempted to distract his critics by arranging for the appointment of a commission to study the problem and recommend changes in the electoral law including the organization of the Central Electoral Board. In December, however, Vásquez had become so disabled by a kidney ailment that he had to visit Johns Hopkins in Baltimore for treatment. In his absence Alfonseca, vice-president since Velásquez's resignation in 1928, was acting president. Appointments to the commission for revision of the electoral law were left to him. The members of the commission were only nominally impartial with the result that the commission's report recommended modifications making the law even more favorable to the party in power.[32]

The opposition centered its criticism on that part of the report concerning changes, or more precisely, the lack of them, in the composition of the Central Electoral Board. The opposition persistently had demanded representation on the Board. The report of the commission rejected this proposal and gave as its reason that the current members of the Board had been appointed to four

---

[32]John Moors Cabot, charge, to Stimson. 10 Jan. 1930. 839.00/3343.

year terms that had not yet expired.[33]

John Moors Cabot, chargé of the Legation after Young's departure in December of 1929, reported that he feared that the opposition would seek redress of its grievances through revolution. He thought its chances of success remote but even unsuccessful disturbances were undesirable. He wrote that he regarded the Legation's task as that of using its influence and prestige to maintain the tranquility that had prevailed in the Republic during the preceding six years.[34] The State Department remained entirely passive and there is no record of any suggestions it may have offered as to how Cabot might best manage this task.

As a first step Cabot looked into the question of reform of the Central Electoral Board in an interview with Manuel de Jesús Troncoso de la Concha, president of the Board. Troncoso, Cabot reported, was the single member of the Board not obviously a partisan Horacista. He was considered to be honest and intelligent even by the opposition. Cabot remarked that he was, nevertheless, ". . . notoriously in favor of any government which happens to be in power."[35] Cabot inquired of Troncoso why the opposition could not be represented on the Board if this would help to ensure a peaceful election. Troncoso replied that the opposition was not a cohesive unit. It was composed of several parties and factions each demanding equal representation. As evidence of

---

[33]Cabot to Stimson. 24 Jan. 1930. 839.00/3345.

[34]*Ibid.*

[35]*Ibid.*

this he pointed out that Desiderio Arias had already made just such a demand for his faction.[36]

Cabot persisted in searching for means to allay the suspicions of the opposition. Troncoso finally proposed that the opposition groups be represented on the Mesas Electorales, the election supervisors at the local polling places. These had not yet been appointed and, he explained, if the opponents of Vásquez could actually observe the ballots being cast perhaps they would be satisfied. Troncoso suggested further that election disputes be decided by the courts rather than by the Central Electoral Board. He promised to take these matters up with Vásquez.[37]

At the same time Cabot moved on another front. Having little faith that Troncoso's proposal to give the courts jurisdiction in disputed elections would find approval, he urged Marin de Moya, Minister of Finance, to press upon Vásquez the need to give the opposition representation on the Central Electoral Board.

By January 24, 1930, Moya could reply that Vásquez, by now returned from the United States and in complete charge of the government in his old manner, viewed the proposal favorably. Vásquez was prepared to offer a position on the Board to Juan Vicini Burgos, Provisional President during the last year of the military occupation. Burgos carried the respect of the entire country and was known to be opposed to the re-election of Vásquez.

---

[36]<u>Ibid</u>.

[37]<u>Ibid</u>.

Cabot carried the news to Burgos who indicated that he was unwilling to accept. Cabot urged him to reconsider. It was a matter of civic duty, he argued, as Burgos' presence on the Board would lessen the danger of revolution. Burgos finally agreed to give the matter his serious consideration.[38] In the end, however, there was no opportunity to appoint him to the Board even had he been willing to accept.

During the first week of February, 1930, Charles Curtis arrived in Santo Domingo to assume his duties as American Minister. He pursued the same goals that Cabot had been trying to achieve. On February 11, Curtis reported that he had been assured by high ranking Dominican government officials that measures would be taken to guarantee free and fair elections.[39] Four days later he could report that the opposition would be granted two seats on the Central Electoral Board.[40]

It would seem from Curtis' first dispatchs that the Legation's hope of removing the major source of revolutionary ferment had been realized since it met one of the principal demands of Vásquez's detractors. No sooner had the government made its announcement, however, than Velásquez announced that his party, the largest single opposition group, would not participate in the elections. Curtis then approached Velásquez seeking an explanation.

---

[38] _Ibid._

[39] Curtis to Stimson. 11 Feb. 1930. 839.00/3346.

[40] Curtis to Stimson. 15 Feb. 1930. 839.00/3347.

Velásquez explained that he personally was opposed to a boycott of the elections and had urged his party to participate with or without representation on the Board. His followers had outvoted him, however, for they believed that the elections would be unfair in spite of the concessions made by the government. They, along with members of other factions, now wanted equal representation on the Mesas Electorales. Curtis informed Velásquez that in his view this too could probably be obtained. Velásquez promised to advise his followers to reconsider their positions. At the same time, however, he told Curtis quite frankly that he did not believe they would heed his advice. Curtis reported to the Department that he doubted that Velásquez would be successful.[41]

It mattered little, for the entire discussion of changes in the various electoral boards was soon to become quite academic. The efforts by Cabot and, after his arrival, Curtis were not misfires. They did as a matter of fact meet with some success. They were able to persuade Vásquez to make certain concessions to his opponents. The Legation's efforts were, however, misdirected. The real threat of revolution came not from vocal dissenters such as Velásquez, but rather from a source close to the government, the commander of the Dominican army, General Rafael Trujillo, and others outside the government whom he found temporarily useful.

This fact was not unknown to the State Department and its representatives in Santo Domingo. Just before he left his post,

---

[41]Curtis to Stimson. 17 Feb. 1930. 839.00.3351.

Young reported, on Christmas day, 1929, that the Dominican political situation was becoming increasingly uncertain. Behind this uncertainty, he wrote, ". . . the attitude of General Trujillo looms as a gigantic question mark upon the backdrop of the Dominican political stage."[42]

Young had been aware for some time that Trujillo, Commander-in-Chief of the Dominican Army, had been scheming with others in a plot to overthrow the government. It was known even this early that Rafael Estrella Urena was deeply involved in a plot against the government and that Velásquez was at least aware of it. Young had taken steps to head off Trujillo's participation. He rightly believed that if the army remained loyal to the government, whatever the others might do stood little chance of success. Accordingly, Young sought out the General and asked him where he stood should a revolution be attempted. Trujillo assured him that in that event he would remain loyal to the government. Young confessed that he could not be certain of the worth of these assurances. He concluded on the following doubtful note:

> It is evident that sudden variations in the political situation must be expected at least until after the elections. No complete stability can exist, and there is a possibility that events may take a serious turn. It is profoundly to be hoped that General Trujillo will abide, in the troublous days ahead, by the assurances which he has given the Legation.[43]

That Trujillo's assurances were worthless soon became apparent. Shortly after Young's dispatch was written the State Department

---

[42]Young to Stimson. 25 Dec. 1929. 839.00/3340.

[43]*Ibid*.

received a revealing report concerning Trujillo's activities from Richard M. Cutts, Colonel, United States Marine Corps, serving at the time as Commander of the Haitian constabulary. Cutts had served in the Dominican constabulary during the occupation and had been instrumental in recruiting Trujillo for officer's training. The two had subsequently become close friends. In early January, 1930, Cutts reported that a group of Dominican officers had paid him a call in Port au Prince. They were touring Haiti, ostensibly, to learn at first hand the reasons for martial law having been recently imposed upon that unhappy country. They explained that as Cutts was the Military Commander their visit to him was a matter of military courtesy.[44]

After a few moments conversation, however, Cutts began to see that they had come to him on behalf of Trujillo. The General wanted Cutts' advice pertaining to the domestic crisis in the Dominican Repulic. They explained that conditions were daily growing worse; that Vásquez was ill and no longer able to control the affairs of government. In Trujillo's judgment, they related, no new president would be elected before August 15, owing to these unstable conditions. In this event the country would be without an executive after that date since Vásquez's term would have expired. Furthermore, even if elections were held before August 15, they would be surrounded by chaos and the results would be meaningless. In either event, General Trujillo believed

---

[44]Report from Port au Prince by Colonel Cutts. Enclosed in: State Dept. dispatch from from Francis White, Asst. Sec. of State, to Cabot. 18 Jan. 1930. 839.00/3341.

that he had a grave responsibility in the matter. The Dominican officers explained to Cutts that Trujillo felt that if events followed their apparent course, he would be forced ". . . to take charge of the situation."[45]

Cutts understood this to mean that Trujillo intended to use the army to seize control of the government. He believed, that owing to their close personal relationship, Trujillo had made his intentions known to him in order to justify whatever action he might have to take. Cutts, in his own words, felt that Trujillo wanted "to play it straight" with him.[46] Trujillo did not "play it straight" with anyone and Cutts flattered himself if he thought he was an exception. It should have been apparent to Cutts that Trujillo's responsibility was not to seize control of the government in case of disturbances. Rather, his assignment was to defend the existing government.

Cutts reported that his response to the visit of the Dominican officers was entirely negative. He had refused to give Trujillo's agents any advice. According to his own account, he told them that the matter was the concern of the Department of State. The extent of his involvement would be to lay Trujillo's case before the American Minister at Santo Domingo.[47]

While Cutts would give no advice to the Dominicans he did offer some to the State Department. He reported that in his

---

[45]*Ibid.*

[46]*Ibid.*

[47]*Ibid.*

judgment Trujillo's assessment of the Dominican political situation was accurate and that Trujillo regarded him, Cutts, too highly to mislead him. He also ascribed pure motives to the action that Trujillo was contemplating. He wrote that Trujillo was already wealthy and did not seek power with that end in view. Nor did he believe that the General was politically ambitious. Cutts professed to believe that Trujillo's only motive was to fulfill his responsibilities as Chief of Staff of the Dominican army. He added that if the circumstances predicted by Trujillo did arise, the General would be ". . . a stabilizing factor beyond ordinary reach.[48]

Certain allowances have to be made for the fact that Cutts, when making these observations, did not have the advantage of hindsight. Even so, his view of Trujillo's motives seems naive. Having been told what Trujillo's intentions were, his conclusion that the General had no political ambitions seems incredibly unsophisticated.

The Department of State was not taken in, however. In forwarding Cutts' report to Cabot, Francis White, Assistant Secretary of State, called attention to the fact that Trujillo was involved in a plot to overthrow the government. Cutts' advice was dismissed as the product of his friendship with Trujillo.[49] Further evidence of this attitude is seen in a department memo concerned with the Cutts report drawn up by Dana G. Munro, Chief

---

[48]<u>Ibid</u>.

[49]White to Cabot. 18 Jan. 1930. 839.00/3341.

of the Latin American Division of the State Department. The memo directed attention only to Trujillo's apparent intention to seize control of the government. Cutts' analysis of his motives was again discounted.[50]

Cabot had his own sources of information which confirmed that Trujillo's assurances that he would remain loyal to the government were worthless. On January 28, he reported that it was generally known in the Republic that Trujillo had ambitions opposed to the Vásquez administration. There had been a great clamor in the press for "reform in the army." This, Cabot explained, was a euphemism calling for the dismissal of Trujillo. There had also been an angry row in the cabinet over whether the General should be ousted.[51] Vásquez, though fully aware that Trujillo was involved in a conspiracy, was opposed to dismissing him at that particular time for he did not wish to risk igniting an immediate coup by the army which he believed would follow. Vásquez preferred to express confidence in Trujillo's loyalty in his public statements and thereby gain time in which to thwart his machinations.[52]

In view of the fact that Cabot and Curtis had been apprised of Trujillo's conspiritorial activities, some explanation would seem to be required for their persistence in trying to maintain tranquility through a compromise between the political disputants

---

[50]Department Memo by Munro. Undated. 839.00/3365.

[51]Cabot to Joseph P. Cotton, Acting Secretary. 38 Jan. 1930. 839.00/3344.

[52]Cabot to Cotton. 10 Jan. 1930. 839.00/3342.

and ignoring the General. In the first place they apparently had no precise information on Trujillo's political connections. They knew that he coveted the presidency. If he meant to have it by an out-and-out army coup there was little that they could do to prevent it. This, however, Trujillo was unlikely to do for it would have united the several political parties and factions against him and he would have found himself in a precarious position. So far as was known, Trujillo had no political support. Perhaps Cabot and, later, Curtis believed that if a political settlement could be reached it would remove any justification Trujillo might think he had for seizing power.

Perhaps Trujillo's machinations simply were not taken seriously enough. This seems to have been the case with Cabot in particular. While he was alert to reports concerning plots against the government, Cabot treated them rather lightly. He apparently believed that Vásquez was shrewd enough to survive an attempted revolution, especially since his health had greatly improved after his treatment at Johns Hopkins.[53] This attitude is revealed by Cabot in his report to the Department of an incident that occurred after Vásquez's return. During his absence, Alfonseca, Moya and Trujillo had all indulged in several petty gambits designed to promote their own interests. Upon his return Vásquez immediately took them to task for their conduct. Cabot described their reaction to the reprimand as that of three school

---

[53]Curtis to Cotton. 11 Feb. 1930. 839.00/3346.

boys ". . . caught by the master in some prank.[54]

Cabot fairly scoffed at the notion that a revolution led by vocal dissenters such as Velásquez could be successful. The latter had been making inflammatory statements criticizing the government in connection with the unfairness of the electoral law. Accordingly, Cabot requested an interview with Velásquez to discover his views and determine what, if anything, might satisfy him. During the interview, Velásquez flatly predicted that a revolution would erupt. For his own part, he claimed to have urged restraint upon his followers, but they no longer listened to him. In his report of this conversation, Cabot observed that Velásquez, though he enjoyed a reputation as a man of peace, was not helping the situation with his "incendiary utterances." As for Velásquez'a gloomy predictions, Cabot recalled that he had made them before and ". . . on no previous occasion has a disaster to the country's peace followed."[55]

On an earlier occasion Cabot had expressed the view that, though the danger that a revolution would be attempted was clear and present, he regarded its chances for success as remote.[56] It is well to point out that in neither of these two instances did Cabot specifically include an army rebellion in his predictions that a revolution would not be successful. On the other hand, he did not qualify his observations in any manner.

---

[54]Cabot to Cotton. 10 Jan. 1930. 839.00/3346.

[55]Cabot to Cotton. 24 Jan. 1930. 839.00/3345.

[56]Cabot to Cotton. 10 Jan. 1930. 839.00/3343.

Charles Curtis was in an unfortunate position for he had arrived at his post less than a month before the revolution broke out. During this time he concentrated his efforts on attempting to mediate the dispute over electoral reform. Keeping abreast of the rapidly changing circumstances from day to day was no small task. It seems logical to conclude, however, that he had been briefed on those events preceding his arrival. It is inconceivable that he had not been informed of Trujillo's intrigue. Until after the revolution had begun, however, his communications to the Department did not reveal what views he may have held on the matter. He hoped, and apparently believed, that his efforts to effect a measure of electoral reform were sufficient to secure a continuation of the domestic peace.

This hopeful note is revealed in his dispatch of February 15, in which he reported that Vásquez had granted the opposition two seats on the Central Electoral Board. He observed that this concession had improved the chances for a peaceful election.[57] Four days earlier he had described the resignation of two former members of the Board, making room for the appointment of two new members favorable to the opposition, as a ". . . victory for moderation and peace."[58]

Curtis was aware that conspiracies other than Trujillo's were in the making. This is evident in his reports concerning

---

[57]Curtis to Cotton. 15 Feb. 1930. 839.00/3347.

[58]Curtis to Cotton. 11 Feb. 1930. 839.00/00 General Conditions/48.

the activities of Elias Brache, the Minister of Justice in Vásquez's cabinet. Brache was not an Horacista; instead he had a small personal following of his own. He had so far supported Vásquez's candidacy but was threatening to join the opposition if Alfonseca were the vice-presidential candidate. He submitted his resignation when it became known that Alfonseca was to receive the nomination. Vásquez refused to accept it and attempted to reach a compromise with Brache. It was arranged that Brache, who had organized a Coalition party for the election, and Vásquez's National Party would present identical lists to the electorate with the exception of the vice-presidential candidate. Brache's party would nominate Angel Morales, also an Horacista, instead of Alfonseca. All other candidates had been agreed upon by Vásquez and Brache.[59]

When Brache made his list public, however, all candidates included in the list originally agreed upon who were supporters of Alfonseca had been removed. In retaliation Vásquez quickly scratched all candidates on his list who had been included at the instance of Brache.[60] Curtis reported that this had been a transparently deliberate attempt on Brache's part to leave Vásquez with no alternative but to accept his resignation. Curtis confessed that he could not fathom what had motivated Brache. He warned the Department, however, to be prepared for even more

---

59Curtis to Cotton. 15 Feb. 1930. 839.00/3347.

60Curtis to Cotton. 16 Feb. 1930. 839.00/3348.

surprising moves by Brache.[61]

It could not be expected that Curtis should have been able to penetrate the precise meaning of Brache's maneuver. Apparently even Vásquez, an astute analyst of his own political domain, was mystified. Brache was adept at political intrigue. Three weeks later, when his liaison with Trujillo had become known, Curtis wrote that Brache had long been known as a political intriguer. He was not as corrupt as some nor as dangerous as others, Curtis continued, but he combined these failings with a lack of principle unsurpassed even in the Dominican Republic.[62]

Earlier, Cabot had reported that during the quarrel in the cabinet over the dismissal of Trujillo, Brache had been a vociferous defender of the General.[63] Again it can only be assumed that Curtis knew of this. It might be argued that in that case he should have related this incident to Brache's resignation and what was generally known of his character. In Curtis' defense it can be said that Trujillo's connections with politicians were veiled by an elaborate secrecy. His contacts with opposition leaders who were plotting revolution were made through civilian go-betweens. His two principal agents were Rafael Vidal, a journalist, and Roberto Despradel, a lawyer, both destined to be of more or less brief prominence after Trujillo became Dictator. This procedure not only served to cover the General's machinations

---

[61]Curtis to Cotton. 17 Feb. 1930. 839.00/3351.

[62]Curtis to Cotton. 7 Mar. 1930. 839.00/3357.

[63]Cabot to Cotton. 28 Jan. 1930. 839.00/3344.

but led the politicians party to the plot to believe that they were in command of the situation and that Trujillo was satisfied with a much needed political base, for he had none of his own.[64]

Whether Curtis should have detected the connection between Trujillo and Brache and other Dominican politicos is another academic point. Knowing of the conspiracy was of little consequence unless he was able to do something to alter its outcome. The State Department, however, when faced with the actual fact of revolution did not alter its policy even slightly from that applied to the circumstances preceding it.

The revolution was largely bloodless and of brief duration, lasting only six days, and was more in the nature of a coup d'etat. This allowed little time for the United States to formulate a new approach even if a new course had been considered desirable. The evidence points to a contrary conclusion: the State Department regarded any more active role on the part of the United States as undesirable. Such measures as Curtis did take were at his own initiative and affected only the means by which the revolution was ended and not its final result.

The revolution began February 22, in Santiago under the leadership of Rafael Estrella Urena. He led a demonstration in front of San Luis fortress, the second largest post of the Dominican army. After a few rounds of small arms fire had been spent in the air, Colonel Simón Díaz, commander of the fort, ordered its

---

[64]German E. Ornes. Trujillo: Little Caesar of the Caribbean. (New York, 1958) p. 47.

surrender and the doors were thrown open to the rebels. They thus acquired a sufficient quantity of arms and ammunition to mount a march on Santo Domingo.[65]

The whole affair, of course, had been carefully arranged in advance. Curtis later learned that Trujillo had been conspiring with Estrella Urena since January 6, at least, and perhaps long before that. Díaz was Trujillo's man and had been following his instructions. To be certain that the rebels acquired sufficient arms by the action at Santiago to present a plausible threat to the government, Trujillo had shipped some of his reserve stock of arms and ammunition from Ozama Fortress in Santo Domingo to the Santiago fortress. Original plans had called for the revolution to begin on February 8, 1930. Curtis, however, had been visiting in Santiago at that time causing its delay.[66]

Curtis first learned of the revolution on the morning of February 24, when Francisco J. Peynado, Secretary of Foreign Affairs, called at the Legation and requested asylum for President and Mrs. Vásquez and Vice-President Alfonseca. Curtis, after being apprised of the conditions then obtaining replied that he failed to see the immediacy of the problem and consented only reluctantly to grant asylum. When Vásquez and a whole entourage of others arrived at the Legation a short time later, Curtis convinced the Dominican president that he should either return

---

[65]Foreign Relations. II. 1930. Curtis to Cotton. 1 Mar. 1930. 839.00 Revolutions/48. p. 170.

[66]Ibid. p. 711.

to the National Palace or take refuge in Ozama Fortress. But by no means should he surrender his office at that untimely moment.[67]

Vásquez doubted that he would find safety in a fort commanded by Trujillo but was assured by Curtis that he was needlessly concerned. Curtis told Vásquez that prior to the arrival of the presidential party he had phoned Trujillo and the General had personally assured him of his loyalty. Later that same day Curtis visited Trujillo at Ozama and was again assured of Trujillo's steadfast determination to defend Vásquez against the rebels. Vásquez was probably not taken in by these assurances of loyalty. He agreed, nevertheless, to do as Curtis had requested and only Mrs. Vásquez remained at the Legation.[68]

Curtis, too, apparently was uncertain as to how much faith to place in Trujillo's professions of loyalty. Later the same morning, after prevailing upon Vásquez to remain in his office, Curtis reported that he viewed as his primary task the prevention, if possible, of the violent overthrow of the government. If, as seemed apparent, Vásquez had to be replaced before the elections, it was to be hoped that the change could be made in an orderly manner, that is, a negotiated resignation. Curtis believed that if the revolutionaries succeeded in ousting him by

---

[67]<u>Ibid.</u> Curtis to Cotton- 24 Feb. 1930 839.00 Revolutions/2. p. 699.

[68]<u>Ibid.</u> Curtis to Acting Sec. Cotton. 1 Mar. 1930. 839.00 Revolutions/48. p. 710.

force the progress in political stability developed over the preceding six years would be lost.[69]

To realize this end Curtis sent Cabot to the rebel stronghold in Santiago to negotiate with Estrella Urena and Elias Brache, whose enigmatic role had by that time been unravelled, and other lesser figures leading the revolution. Cabot was authorized to make two concessions to the revolutionaries if they would agree not to expand their operations. First, Alfonseca would resign from the vice-presidency and agree not to stand for re-election. Secondly, all amendments made to the electoral law since 1924 would be annulled.[70] This was an explicit recognition by Curtis that the revolution could not be suppressed entirely and that some rebel demands would have to be met. Implicit in his willingness to go this far was the recognition that Vásquez would very likely have to be replaced by a provisional president more amenable to the demands of the leaders of the revolution. Vásquez had already admitted this when he sought asylum at the Legation. Had the loyalty of the army been dependable, it would not have been necessary to go this far to accommodate the revolutionaries.

In sending Cabot to treat with Estrella Urena, Curtis did temporarily confuse the conspiracy to overthrow Vásquez. It incidentally uncovered Trujillo's involvement in the plot and

---

[69]Ibid. Curtis to Acting Sec. Cotton. 24 Feb. 1930. 839.00 Revolutions/3. p. 699.

[70]Ibid. p. 699.

removed any doubts that Curtis may still have entertained concerning the worth of the General's assurances of loyalty.

Cabot, after establishing contact with Estrella Urena, obtained from him a promise not to advance on the capital city until he, Cabot, had returned there to present the rebel demands to Vásquez. These demands were four in number. First, the appointment of a Secretary of Interior satisfactory to both the government and the rebels was called for. Secondly, Vásquez was then to resign after designating the new Secretary of Interior as acting, or provisional, president. In his turn the provisional president would appoint a balanced cabinet. Third, the electoral law of 1924 was to be re-enacted. Finally, Vásquez, but not Alfonseca, could be a candidate in the presidential election still scheduled to take place in May.[71]

The appearance of Cabot on the scene caused a delay in the rebel plans to march on Santo Domingo. Estrella Urena had promised not to do so until a reply to his demands had been received from Vásquez, a promise to be broken but not in time to prevent Trujillo's participation in the plot from becoming known.

Before Cabot could return to the capital, Curtis had been informed that the revolutionary forces had advanced to the outskirts of the city. Curtis phoned Trujillo to get a confirmation of this report. The General not only confirmed that the rebel army had arrived but with its greater numbers had outflanked the

---

[71]Ibid. Curtis to Acting Sec. Cotton. 26 Feb. 1930. 839.00 Revolutions/19.

government troops. When, however, the revolutionary forces had not entered the city by six o'clock on the morning of February 25, Curtis drove out to the positions of the government troops to investigate the situation for himself. The field commander of this force, Colonel José Alfonseca, a distant relative of the vice-president, informed Curtis that the revolutionary leaders had apparently kept their promise to Cabot. Not only was the government force not outflanked but so far as Colonel Alfonseca could determine, the revolutionaries were still in their positions in and around Santiago.[72]

This condition proved to be shortlived as the revolutionary army did move on the capital that night. The delay in their plans, however, revealed conclusively that Trujillo could not be trusted. He had misled Curtis concerning the whereabouts of the rebel force because he believed that it was or soon would be where he said it was. He had not yet learned of Curtis' attempts to effect a negotiated settlement and, quite apparently, had not been informed by Estrella Urena that a delay in the advance on Santo Domingo had been made necessary.

In the meantime, Cabot had returned to the capital and reported the results of his meeting with the revolutionaries leading Curtis to cable the Department that he believed there was a good chance for a peaceful settlement. As a precautionary measure, however, he had requested that a naval vessel be sent

---

[72]*Ibid.* Curtis to Act. Sec. Cotton. 1 Mar. 1930. 839.00 Revolutions/48. p. 710.

to Dominican waters without delay. So far there had been no evidence of hostility toward Americans, he reported. Nor did he believe that either the government or the rebel forces represented a potential danger. He did fear that unorganized street fighting might erupt in Santo Domingo to threaten American lives and property. A naval vessel on the sight would discourage this.[73]

The Department of State refused to consider this procedure. Joseph P. Cotton, Acting Secretary of State throughout this affair, replied that vessels were already stationed in nearby areas, Puerto Rico and Cuba. These might be called upon to deal with an actual threat to American lives, or if the customs service were interfered with, or in the event of "substantial" destruction of property. No vessels would be sent, however, unless and until the danger was clear and present.[74]

This was the clearest policy statement made by the Department up to this point of the crisis and it illustrates the attitude of the Hoover administration outlined above. There was great reluctance to take any action reminiscent of intervention. Intervention, in the form of sending warships to the Dominican Republic, might be undertaken, however, if actual depradations against Americans, their property or the receivership did occur.

At this same time the State Department, which had so far been silent as to what Curtis should do, forwarded instructions.

---

[73] Ibid. Curtis to Cotton. 25 Feb. 1930. 839.00 Revolutions/14. p. 702.

[74] Ibid. Cotton to Curtis. 25 Feb. 1930. 839.00 Revolutions/13. p. 701.

Curtis was limited in how far he could go in his efforts to avert a violent overthrow of the government. As indicated above, he could not put any kind of pressure on the Dominicans that implied in any way the use of force. On February 26, Curtis received specific instructions concerning how he should conduct himself in meeting the crisis. He was authorized ". . . to be of any assistance which might be welcomed by the Dominican political leaders in attempting to bring about an agreement for the peaceful and orderly arrangement of present difficulties.[75]

This would seem to indicate that even friendly counsel should be withheld if the Dominicans regarded it as offensive. This view of the intent of Curtis' instructions is confirmed in a telegram that Curtis had received earlier in the day explaining his instructions. He was told that he could use or not use his instructions as his discretion directed him. Under no circumstances, however, was he to make any formal communications to the Dominican government concerning the matter encompassed by those instructions.[76] In other words he could offer the friendly counsel of the Legation but he was not authorized to submit any proposal as having the support of the United States government. Any suggestions that Curtis might make were to be presented as his own and not those of the government he represented.

---

[75]Ibid. Cotton to Curtis. 26 Feb. 1930. 839.00 Revolutions/35. p. 704.

[76]Ibid. Cotton to Curtis. 26 Feb. 1930. 839.00 Revolutions/21. pp. 703-704.

Cotton, nevertheless, approved the measures Curtis had initiated in an attempt to mediate between the warring factions. Cotton wished him every success but whatever he might accomplish had to be done without any show of force. If successful under this condition, he continued, it ". . . would materially strengthen our position in the Dominican Republic and in the rest of Latin America." Cotton allowed that Curtis' efforts might not succeed but it was the only prudent course.[77]

The effort to mediate the differences between the Vásquez government and the rebel leaders succeeded to the extent that further violence was averted. This was possible only because the demands of the revolutionaries were met in full. Vásquez agreed to the four prerequisites presented to him through Cabot. As a counter proposal he suggested that Angel Morales be appointed Secretary of the Interior and provisional president until the election and inauguration of a constitutional executive. He also proposed that all arms except those of the national army be turned over to the government.[78]

Even before these proposals could be made known to Estrella Urena his revolutionary army had moved into positions around Santo Domingo during the night of February 25 in complete disregard of the promises made to Cabot. By eight o'clock the next

---

[77]*Ibid*. Cotton to Curtis. 25 Feb. 1930. 839.00 Revolutions/13. pp. 701-702.

[78]*Ibid*. Curtis to Cotton. 26 Feb. 1930. 839.00 Revolutions/19. p. 703.

morning they had filtered into the outskirts of the city itself.[79] The rebels had gone around and through the government positions outside the capital without opposition. Trujillo had arranged for this by relieving Colonel Alfonseca of his command and replacing him with Colonel Simón Díaz who had followed orders so well at Santiago three days earlier. This maneuver, Curtis observed wryly, ". . . at least relieved the Legation of any anxiety concerning the possibility of bloodshed between the Government and revolutionary forces."[80]

With the presence of the rebels in Santo Domingo Curtis again had to exert himself to prevent Vásquez from resigning immediately. Vásquez rightly believed that without any military support--and after Colonel Alfonseca's dismissal he had none--he could not hope to influence the course of negotiations with Estrella Urena. He wanted to resign at once. It was all that Curtis could do to persuade him to remain in his office until an orderly transfer of authority could be arranged. He explained to Vásquez that his resignation would terminate constitutional government and serious disorders would likely ensue. More, perhaps, than any other Dominican, Vásquez was sincerely concerned for the welfare of his country. He put his pride and ambition aside for the moment and acceded to Curtis' advice.[81]

---

[79] _Ibid_. Curtis to Cotton. 26 Feb. 1930. 839.00 Revolutions/16. p. 702.

[80] _Ibid_. Curtis to Cotton. 1 Mar. 1930. 839.00 Revolutions/48. p. 711.

[81] _Ibid_. pp. 711-712.

Curtis was anxious to arrange an agreement soon and before Vásquez could change his mind. The first step was to obtain a pledge from the revolutionary forces not to advance further into the city. He directed Cabot to locate Estrella in order that negotiations might be undertaken. Cabot searched throughout the night of February 25 and early morning hours of the twenty-sixth but found only General José Estrella, field commander of the rebel army and an uncle to Rafael Estrella Urena. General Estrella promised to hold his troops in their positions until it could be determined whether an arrangement for the orderly transfer of power could be agreed upon.[82]

This pledge proved no more sacred than previous ones as later that same day, February 26, the army of the revolution moved into the heart of Santo Domingo. Frustrated by this latest failure of the revolutionaries to observe their commitments, Curtis requested General Estrella to come to the Legation and explain why he had not kept his troops in their positions as he had promised. The General blithely explained that he had been forced to advance in response to an attack by the government forces. Ever alert to the ludicrous, Cabot pointed out that the government forces to which General Estrella had referred was commanded by Colonel Díaz who had manifested his sympathy for the rebel cause in spectacular fashion. It seemed clear, the General was told, that whatever had occurred was the result of collusion on the part

---

[82] Ibid. p. 712.

of the opposing commanders.[83]

With the rebel army now in the streets of Santo Domingo, it was imperative that an agreement between the rebel leaders and the government be reached regarding control of the city. Cabot had been unable to locate Estrella Urena and in his absence a meeting had been arranged between Vásquez and General Estrella. Curtis, who was present at this meeting, reported that Vásquez agreed to the demands made previously by Estrella Urena. General Estrella, on his part, agreed not to attack the presidential mansion and to use his troops to maintain order in the city.[84]

Curtis, having in mind the inconstancy of the rebels in keeping their commitments, had Cabot continue his search for Estrella Urena in order that a conference between the leader of the revolution and Vásquez might be arranged and a final settlement agreed upon. Cabot succeeded in locating the revolutionary leader during the afternoon of February 26. Estrella Urena agreed to come to the Legation that evening. When he failed to appear Cabot sought him out once again. Estrella Urena this time agreed to come to the Legation at eight o'clock the next morning, February 27. On this occasion he kept his appointment.[85]

Curtis had arranged for Vásquez to come to the Legation to confer with Estrella Urena on the means of restoring peace. Vásquez had already resigned himself to the fact that he would

---

[83]Ibid. p. 713.

[84]Ibid. p. 713.

[85]Ibid. p. 714.

have to consent to whatever terms his adversary demanded and had already agreed to those so far presented. Curtis did not sit in on the discussions, even though they were held in the American Legation, but he was kept informed of their progress.[86]

Vásquez and Estrella Urena met twice at the Legation on February 27 and further discussions were held at the Presidential Mansion during the following three days. The basis of an agreement was reached the first day. It was agreed that the electoral law of 1924 would be re-enacted. It was also agreed that all arms held by groups other than the national army would be delivered to the new provisional government that was to be established. It was stipulated that there were to be no restrictions, as to presidential candidates in the May elections with two exceptions. Neither Alfonseca nor Trujillo could be candidates of any party.[87] Both sides were probably pleased with Trujillo's elimination. Vásquez exacted a measure of revenge and Estrella Urena rid himself of a competitor--or so he may have hoped. Other agreements were reached but were concerned with procedures of governmental operations and are of little interest here.

It was not until the second meeting at the Legation on February 27, that agreement was reached on the person to be appointed Secretary of Interior. It has been mentioned that Vásquez had hoped to see Angel Morales, a loyal Horacista, appointed to the post. This was unsatisfactory to Estrella Urena.

---

[86]*Ibid*. p. 714.

[87]*Ibid*. p. 715.

He had arrived early for the second conference and had asked Curtis how the suggestion of appointing Trujillo to this post would be received. Curtis replied that under no circumstances would he recommend recognition by the United States if the new government were headed by the General.[88]

Though he did not strictly exceed his instructions, Curtis did, in this exchange, make use of a diplomatic bluff. He knew full well that a recommendation by him not to recognize a government headed by Trujillo stood little chance of gaining the approval of the Department. He had recommended earlier that Trujillo not be allowed to become either provisional president or a candidate for the presidency in the forthcoming elections. He gave as his reason the General's betrayal of solemn assurances repeatedly given that he would remain loyal to the government.[89] Cotton's reply could hardly be described as encouraging. He stated merely that the situation had not "sufficiently developed" to call for any explicit instructions.[90]

Whether in accord with the spirit of his instructions or not, the bluff worked. Estrella Urena, after obtaining Curtis' view, went into a separate room with Vásquez and they arrived at an agreement. Estrella Urena was to be appointed Secretary of the

---

[88]*Ibid*. p. 714.

[89]*Ibid*. Curtis to Cotton. 26 Feb. 1930. 839.00 Revolutions/20. pp. 704-705.

[90]*Ibid*. Cotton to Curtis. 26 Feb. 1930. 839.00 Revolutions/22. p. 705.

Interior and, subsequently, to be sworn in as provisional president. Curtis was displeased with this decision. In his report to the Department he observed that by appointing the leader of the revolution to this important post the Dominicans were setting an evil precedent. He made his view known to Vásquez and Estrella Urena, but acquiesced in the decision because Vásquez and his advisers told him that Estrella was the only one capable of re-establishing peace and order.[91]

Curtis was consoled also by the fact that the appointment had followed all required legal formalities. He reported that he had told the Dominicans that, owing to the observance of constitutional procedures, there would be no question raised by the United States concerning recognition of the new government.[92] Cotton replied that the Department fully concurred in this view.[93]

With this settlement the first phase of the revolution came to an end. The policy of the State Department throughout the crisis was, in the main, negative and passive. The communications to its representatives at Santo Domingo consisted very largely of mere acknowledgments of dispatches received. The single instruction that it sent to Curtis after the revolution had begun, limited him to the use of his good offices to mediate between the rebels and the government. This Curtis had been doing even before the

---

[91]Ibid. Curtis to Cotton. 26 Feb. 1930. 839.00 Revolutions /32. p. 708.

[92]Ibid. p. 708.

[93]Ibid. Curtis to Cotton. 26 Feb. 1930. 839.00 Revolutions/20. p. 705.

revolution erupted.

The near indifference of the State Department resulted from two major considerations. First, the worldwide economic depression overshadowed all other foreign policy issues. The energies of the United States government were concentrated on domestic issues growing out of the depression. In the field of foreign affairs the economic conditions in Europe were of greater concern than what at the time must have appeared to be just another comic opera military coup in a small Caribbean Republic. The Hoover administration did not wish to expend its energies or the resources at its disposal in an affair, the outcome of which hardly seemed of vital concern when compared to other crises facing it.

Secondly, the policy pursued relative to the Dominican revolution of 1930 was entirely in line with that followed since 1924. Since that time the United States had shown no inclination to interfere with Dominican domestic affairs as long as these presented no threat to American lives or property and did not disrupt the operation of the customs receivership. That was precisely the attitude taken in the revolution of 1930.

For his part, Charles Curtis was prepared to adopt a stronger policy. His recommendations to the Department during the brief revolution are indicative of this. As events developed in the Republic and it became ever more apparent that Trujillo, as a candidate for the presidency, was going to reap the benefits of revolution, Curtis urged an increasingly forceful policy upon the State Department. The latter proved even less willing to involve itself in Trujillo's "election" than it had been to interfere with the outcome of the revolution that had made it possible. It is in the conflicting views held by Curtis on the one hand, and the State Department on the other that the major tenents of the policy of the United States were to become more sharply defined during the months following the revolution.

CHAPTER V

THE ELECTION OF 1930

It was only a short time before it became clear that the arrangement ending the revolution was not to be taken too seriously. The arrangement between Vásquez and Estrella had placed the latter in the presidency in accordance with constitutional provisions applicable to the situation. Estrella, however, could not have extracted those concessions from Vásquez had he not been supported by Trujillo and his army. Curtis did not believe that a revolution would have been attempted had that support not been guaranteed beforehand.[1] Estrella was now faced with the task of subjecting the army to his control or it would be his undoing just as it had been for Vásquez.

That Trujillo intended to capture the leadership of the revolution for himself became apparent very early after Vásquez had agreed to step down. Part of the agreement reached between Vásquez and Estrella was that Trujillo, along with Alfonseca, would not become a candidate for the presidency. As early as March 1, however, Curtis had warned that he believed Trujillo would be a candidate in spite of this agreement.[2]

He confirmed this view a few days later, on March 6, in his summary of the results of the revolution submitted to the Department for its consideration. First, he observed, the success of

---

[1]For. Rel. II. 1930. Curtis to Cotton. 1 Mar. 1930. 839.00 Revolutions/48. p. 711.

[2]*Ibid*. p. 717.

the revolution had set a very bad precedent, as it would encourage other politically ambitious Dominicans to seek satisfaction of their longings for power in the same manner. Already Curtis was hearing on all sides that the recent violence was merely the first in a series of disorders.[3]

A further result of the revolution, and one closely related to the first, was the setback it had given to the continued progress of political stability. For all of its faults, wrote Curtis, the Vásquez government had been a united one strengthened by a broadly based political party. During the six years preceding the revolution it had provided the republic with a much needed stability. The government of Estrella, on the other hand, was divided and weak, composed of unreliable elements already showing signs of disloyalty. Curtis did not expect that Estrella could hold the various factions together through the elections. Furthermore, even though the electoral law of 1924, nearly perfect in its drafting, had been reenacted, Estrella would be unable to ensure its enforcement.[4]

A third result of the revolution, and for the immediate future the most significant, had been the entrance of the army into politics. The danger that this would occur had been foreseen by those with insight into Latin American politics.

---

[3]Curtis to Cotton. 6 Mar. 1930. 839.00/3356.

[4]Ibid.

Writing in 1928, Sumner Welles had observed,

> It is only in the past four years that a new concept of the functions of the military forces in the Republic has developed. The . . . undisciplined . . . army of the old days has developed into the national constabulary . . . a well trained, well organized, well disciplined body . . . more potent than the old army ever was. The elements of danger, therefore, are ever present. Should those who compose this force ever become convinced that their promotion or well-being depends more upon political favour than upon their own efficiency and . . . excellence, the safety of the Republic itself will be jeopardized.[5]

If further proof were needed that national constabularies trained by the United States would not guarantee political stability in the Caribbean Republics, it is provided in the example of the Dominican revolution of 1930. The principle of the separation of the military from politics taught at West Point and Annapolis has never greatly impressed the Latin American military mind.

The very worst consequences of Welles' warning were realized in the Dominican Republic. Curtis complained that the efficient and disciplined army that the United States had trained during the occupation had been fully adequate to defend the government during the recent revolution. Instead, its commander had chosen to use it for a different purpose--his own political ascendancy. Curtis had now learned that already the army was exerting pressure on the electorate to gather support for Trujillo even before his candidacy had been announced officially.[6]

---

[5]Welles. Naboth's Vineyard. II. p. 908.

[6]Curtis to Cotton. 8 Mar. 1930. 839.00/3358.

That Trujillo intended to be a candidate for the presidency in the May election was now clear. On March 6, Curtis made this known to the Department. Indicative of this, Curtis wrote, was Trujillo's increasing domination over the government nominally headed by Estrella. He dictated who was to be appointed to and dismissed from office solely on the basis of their support of or opposition to his candidacy. Since Trujillo had no following or support outside of the army, which could provide few votes, Curtis feared that he would use military force to intimidate the opposition candidates and the electorate. Curtis concluded, "If General Trujillo succeeds in his desire to be president, it seems likely that the Dominican Republic will have to endure a prolonged dictatorship."[7]

As Trujillo's intentions became clear, Curtis urged with increasing vigor that the United States use its influence to prevent his election. The Department of State, on the other hand, rejected all measures that would imply in any way that the United States was interfering in Dominican domestic affairs. The differences between Curtis and the Department of State concerning what should be done to thwart Trujillo's political ambitions bring into sharp focus the problem confronting the United States in its Dominican relations.

On March 18, 1930, Curtis informed the Department that Trujillo had received the presidential nomination of a coalition party formed by the merger of the parties of Estrella and Elias

---

[7]Curtis to Cotton. 6 Mar. 1930. 839.00/3356.

Brache and called the Confederación. Estrella had received the vice-presidential nomination which he accepted reluctantly and only after his request to withdraw his name had been rejected. Estrella felt cheated because he had been unable to obtain the top place on the ticket. This, of course, was the explanation for his reluctance to accept the vice-presidential nomination. His disappointment was given expression in other more meaningful ways. After Trujillo had been nominated, Estrella, who was still provisional president, sought out Curtis and told him that Trujillo had used the army to gain complete dominance over the government. He contended there was no possibility that the elections would be fair. Estrella wanted Curtis to announce that the United States would not recognize Trujillo if he were elected because his candidacy was in violation of the agreement of February 28.[8]

That Curtis was willing to oblige is apparent from his comment regarding Estrella's suggestion. He predicted that if Trujillo were not eliminated a revolution would surely follow his election. "This," he added, "cannot be accomplished by the President (Estrella). Will the Department make any statement on the subject or authorize the Legation to do so? Prompt reply urgently requested."[9]

The reply was prompt--it came the next day, March 19--and

---

[8] For. Rel. II. 1930. Curtis to Cotton. 18 Mar. 1930. 839.00/3355. p. 718.

[9] *Ibid.* p. 718.

the answer was negative. Cotton stated explicitly that Curtis would not be authorized to make any statement to the effect that Trujillo, if elected, would not be recognized. The Department, Cotton informed Curtis,

> . . . expects to recognize Trujillo or any other person coming into office as a result of the coming elections and will maintain the most friendly relations with him and his Government and will desire to cooperate with him in every proper way.[10]

By scrupulously avoiding even the appearance of interference, Cotton added, the United States could continue to enjoy the goodwill resulting from the sound policy pursued during the previous six years.[11]

Cotton stated that he agreed with Curtis that it was regrettable that Trujillo was using his position in the army for his own political advancement. The only means that he would approve to prevent this, however, were appeals by Curtis to Trujillo's patriotism. Curtis was authorized to urge upon Trujillo, confidentially and in a "most friendly manner," as his personal advice the view that the General might damage the political development of his country if he persisted in standing for election. Cotton believed that this method was the only one that stood any chance of success. It would serve no useful purpose to issue a public statement opposing Trujillo, he observed, for this would help rather than injure his candidacy. Curtis should also take

---

[10]*Ibid.* Cotton to Curtis. 19 Mar. 1930. 839.00/3355. p. 718-*719.*

[11]*Ibid.* p. 718.

care, Cotton warned, not to impair his own personal relations with Trujillo in case he was elected.[12]

The clearest statement by Curtis of his views came a few days later on March 31, in his reply to the Department's instructions. He stated explicitly on this occasion that he saw merit in the suggestion made by Estrella which he had earlier forwarded to the Department. His principal reason for favoring the threat not to recognize Trujillo, Curtis stated, was that he believed that the General was so unpopular that his election would be followed by disorders such as those prevailing in 1916. He predicted that within two years after his election the United States would have to intervene to restore order just as it had then. This unwanted eventuality would be avoided if Trujillo could be forced to withdraw his candidacy by making it known that, if elected, he would not be recognized by the United States.[13]

There were three obvious weaknesses in this argument. In the first place, Curtis was attempting to recommend a policy for the prevention of circumstances which were by no means certain to arise. He had, as a matter of fact, previously predicted a prolonged dictatorship if Trujillo were elected.[14] Even had he been correct in predicting disturbances, it was at least doubtful that the United States would take the measures that he foresaw.

---

[12]Ibid. pp. 718-719.

[13]Curtis to Cotton. 31 Mar. 1930. 839.00 Presidential Campaigns/ 10.

[14]See above: p. 147. footnote 7.

Secondly, his proposal to interfere with the election by opposing Trujillo's candidacy might have brought on the very disorders that he hoped to prevent. The disorders that had occurred in the period 1911-1916 were the result, in part at least, of the efforts by the United States to impose a solution unsatisfactory to the Dominicans. Thirdly, it had been made clear to Curtis that what he proposed was not at all in keeping with the general aims of the United States in Latin America.

Curtis did defend his position with other more telling arguments, however. He advised the Department that its suggestion that he persuade Trujillo to withdraw his candidacy by appealing to his patriotism was less than useless. The Department's estimate of Trujillo's character apparently differed from his own, Curtis wrote, and added,

> . . . the Legation believes that General Trujillo is entirely selfish and lacking in patriotism, that he sees that he is in a position to force the country to accept him as its President and that it may well happen that he will never again be in that position, so it behooves him to seize the present opportunity.[15]

Curtis' estimate of the situation on this score can hardly be disputed. On the other hand, Cotton, even though it had been he who had suggested the appeal to Trujillo's best instincts, did not really believe that it would be successful and he had made this clear to Curtis.[16] It was not, however, as one account

---

[15]Curtis to Cotton. 31 Mar. 1930. 839.00 Presidential Campaigns/10.

[16]For. Rel. II. 1930. Cotton to Curtis. 19 Mar. 1930. 839.00/3355. p. 719.

contends, a matter of "appeasing" Trujillo.[17] Cotton's suggestion was, as he saw it, the only means by which the United States could express its attitude concerning Trujillo's election and at the same time stay clear of the charge of having tampered with Dominican domestic affairs. This was precisely the position taken by the State Department when Vásquez extended his presidential term and later decided to stand for re-election.

In further defense of his position Curtis argued that the very credibility of the position of the United States vis-a-vis Trujillo was at stake. He contended that if the United States failed to oppose Trujillo it could retain neither its own self-respect nor that of Trujillo. He had broken every promise he had ever made to the Legation and continued to prevaricate in his dealings with it to that very hour. Curtis continued,

> The Legation can never again feel any confidence in General Trujillo, whatever the outward appearances may be, but he, however much he may dislike or resent the Legation's attitude, must continue to feel respect for its principles.[18]

It was Curtis' contention that if Trujillo were allowed to believe that he could continue to treat the representatives of the government of the United States in this fashion it would be difficult to deal with him in the future. If he found that he could ignore any commitments he might make to the American Minister, the Legation would not be very useful as a means of

---

[17]German E. Ornes. Trujillo: Little Caesar of the Caribbean. (New York, 1958). p. 47.

[18]Curtis to Cotton. 31 Mar. 1930. 839.00 Presidential Campaigns/10.

instituting a Dominican policy. It was to Curtis' credit that he foresaw this problem. One of the difficulties that the United States would have with Trujillo during the 1930's was his inclination to maintain his relations with it outside the normal channels of communication. He utilized his acquaintances in the Marine Corps; he attempted, and on occasion succeeded, to suborn American journalists and national legislators; he paid extraordinary fees to private American citizens, all to lobby in his interest at the highest levels of the executive branch of government in the United States. His persistent use of these avenues of communication, particularly the latter, made it difficult to coordinate the work of the State Department and its officers in Santo Domingo. Trujillo would use succeeding American ministers just as he had Curtis until they too became disillusioned, at which point he would bypass them.

In further support of his recommendations that Trujillo not be recognized, Curtis raised a point that struck at the very heart of a dilemma in which the United States found itself on this occasion and which continues to challenge one aspect of its Latin American policy to the present. The United States has been accused of favoring right-wing dictatorships of either a military or civilian character in Latin America because these have been inclined to support American policies. On the other hand, when the United States has offered resistance to the imposition of such regimes, it has been charged with interfering in the domestic affairs of Latin American countries.

In the Dominican Republic in 1930, this dilemma lay squarely in the path of United States policy. The State Department had chosen not to leave itself open to the charge of interfering in the Dominican election. In defense of his conduct, which had been markedly unfriendly toward Trujillo, Curtis pointed out that as a result of this policy Trujillo was considered a great friend of the United States and, ". . . had the Legation continued to show itself . . . cordial to him . . . the country would have seen in him an instrument of American oppression."[19] Curtis recognized that the prestige of the United States would suffer if it interfered to prevent Trujillo's election. It would suffer equally, however, if Trujillo were elected and, Curtis added, this would have been the case even had ". . . the Legation assumed no attitude at all."[20]

The Dominican politicians were as much aware of the dilemma as was Curtis and they calculated this factor into their own maneuvers. They deliberately sought to draw the United States into their affairs when this seemed to be their political advantage. Perhaps too late Curtis began to see this quite clearly.

On March 31, he wrote to the Department explaining that it had become increasingly evident that Estrella and Brache had bought Trujillo's betrayal of Vásquez with the promise that he would be the presidential candidate of a party organized by them

---

[19]<u>Ibid</u>.

[20]<u>Ibid</u>.

for that purpose. At the first opportunity--during the negotiations ending the revolution--they then betrayed Trujillo by agreeing to his elimination as a candidate.[21] That they had counted upon the support of the United States to enforce this agreement is evident from the fact that Estrella had sought Curtis' view of Trujillo's candidacy before coming to an agreement with Vásquez. It is seen again when, after Trujillo had received the nomination, Estrella requested that Curtis announce the intention of the United States not to recognize a government headed by him.[22]

Brache, of course, was aiming for the double double-cross. He had been present at the meeting between Vásquez and Estrella when terms were agreed upon ending the revolution. He was as well a party to the commitment eliminating Trujillo as a presidential candidate. It was Brache, however, who had arranged Trujillo's nomination on March 18.[23] This effectively removed Estrella as a possible rival. Brache was counting upon pressure from the United States to force Trujillo to withdraw. Curtis explained that Brache then intended to place his own name at the head of the ticket.[24]

When, however, it was learned that the United States would

---

[21]<u>Ibid</u>.

[22]See above; page 148. footnote 9.

[23]<u>For. Rel.</u> II. 1930. Curtis to Cotton. 21 Mar. 1930. 839.00/3359. p. 720.

[24]Curtis to Cotton. 11 Apr. 1930. 839.00/3368.

not interfere in the election as Brache and Estrella had anticipated, they immediately began to make their peace with Trujillo. Estrella did a complete about face and began denouncing the candidates of the Alianza[25] for conspiring to defeat Trujillo by seeking the intervention of the United States.[26] This not only served to blacken the reputation of Trujillo's opponents but portrayed the General as the defender of the honor of the Republic against the ambitions of the Northern Colossus.

Perhaps this entire matter was most intelligently summarized by a young Dominican writer, Angel Martinez. Curtis forwarded to the Department an article written by him and presented it as representative of the views of many intelligent Dominicans. Martinez began by running down the list of evils suffered by Dominicans since the onset of the revolution and blamed them on the ambitions of the Republic's politicians. Dominicans, he wrote, should not consider it a crime to ask Washington to be of help in matters affecting their domestic affairs. They should not fear American aid in order to establish an impartial provisional government and to remove Trujillo from control of the army.[27]

This view, he confessed, was not highly patriotic, but it invited no greater interference than that usually conceded to

---

[25]A coalition of the National and Progresista Parties. Its candidates were Frederico Velásquez and Angel Morales for the presidency and vice-presidency respectively.

[26]Curtis to Stimson. 6 May 1930. 839.00/3402.

[27]Curtis to Stimson. 24 May 1930. 839.00/3413.

the United States. "Everyone," Martinez continued, "has his own way of desiring the aid of the United States, and provided that it suits his convenience or is carried out in accordance with his own preferences, he sees no reason to fear it."[28]

Martinez went on to predict a return to the chaos that had provoked intervention in 1916. Regrettable though interference might be, he wrote,

> . . . at least the advice of our powerful neighbors would accomplish the miracle of giving us the necessary strength to block the mad ambitions which closed the hearts of our politicians to the desires of the people.[29]

Martinez--and those whose views he represented--were as much affected by the attitude he had described as were his fellow citizens. As he had written, everyone had his own reasons for wanting interference by the United States. Martinez may have welcomed the help of the United States in ridding the country of Trujillo. This suited his preference and he did not "fear it." It is problematical how he may have reacted to any solution arising out of intervention. Very likely the United States would have been blamed for any unhappy results.

Illustrative of this point is the fact that Martinez was already laying part of the blame for the conditions existing in 1930 at the feet of the United States, or at least, its representative in Santo Domingo. Curtis had, according to Martinez,

---

[28]*Ibid.*

[29]*Ibid.*

". . . contrary to precedents set in similar cases by the American Chancery, permitted the revolution to obtain the power to satisfy the excessive ambitions of an unscrupulous group. . . ." Though unfair to him, Curtis remarked only that the Martinez article was "somewhat incorrect" in some particulars.[30]

Though his recommendations had been rejected, Curtis continued to forward to the Department reports of the election campaign unfavorable to Trujillo. On March 17, he reported that a strong political force opposed to Trujillo's election was being forged. It consisted primarily of Vásquez's Partido Nacional, which was recovering from the demoralization that had set in after the revolution and the retirement of its leader from public life. Alfonseca still had influence in the party but had expressed a willingness to allow other less controversial figures with broader support to take over the leadership. The National Party alone could still command fifty per cent of the electorate, and the formation of a coalition with one or more of the other parties was only a matter of time. Curtis observed that when this occurred Trujillo would have no chance whatsoever of winning a fair election. He added, however, that Trujillo intended to use violence and intimidation to win. If these did not succeed, it was believed that he would seize the presidency by force.[31]

Trujillo's methods of arranging his electoral victory were not confined to stuffing the ballot boxes. He put the army to

---

[30]*Ibid.*

[31]Curtis to Cotton, 17 Mar. 1930, 839.00/3360.

use early to intimidate the opposition. A patrol of military personnel ambushed an automobile carrying some leaders of the Progresista Party, by then in coalition with the National Party.[32] Earlier he had ordered the army to seize all firearms in the Republic. The most flagrant example of this was seen on an occasion when a number of Dominican senators were visiting President Estrella--at his invitation--at the National Palace. During the fête the army moved in and seized the hand weapons carried by the Senators' chauffeurs.[33]

The army, Curtis reported, was moving all over the country instead of concentrating in the areas specified by the electoral law. Soldiers dressed as civilians were shooting at the opposition and in general causing disturbances in an effort either to intimidate the electorate or to create a pretext which would justify the army in taking over control of the government.[34]

These attacks on the population were, wrote Curtis, simply outrageous. Assassinations and kidnappings were committed daily by the officers and men of the army and Trujillo was responsible.[35] Although, in accordance with the Constitution, he had taken a leave of absence in order to run for the presidency, Trujillo was still effectively in control of the army. On April 5, Curtis reported that the General, in order to counter

---

[32]Curtis to Cotton. 5 Apr. 1930. 839.00/3360.

[33]Curtis to Cotton. 25 Mar. 1930. 839.00/3364.

[34]Curtis to Cotton. 18 Apr. 1930. 839.00/3374.

[35]Curtis to Cotton. 5 Apr. 1930. 839.00/3370.

the charge that he was using the army to win the election, had issued orders that the commanders of military districts were to refrain from any participation in political activities. Curtis observed,

> It is interesting to note that General Trujillo was officially on leave of absence when the order was given and also that there is not the slightest indication that the officers addressed have paid attention to his order.[36]

At the same time, Curtis had reported that the army was overthrowing the municipal councils and replacing them with councils whose support of Trujillo was assured. This was necessary, Curtis explained, because the councils controlled the local police. Control over local police was important for the election period since the army, according to the electoral law, was forbidden to perform any police function during this period.[37]

Curtis had revised his view concerning the possibility of an outright military coup. He was now certain that elections would be held although there was no possibility that they would be fairly conducted. If it were at all possible, he reported, Trujillo would become president with some semblance of constitutionality in order to be assured of recognition by the United States. "A revolution may precede or follow them," Curtis wrote, "serious disorders are certain, but 'elections' will be held."[38]

---

[36]Curtis to Cotton. 5 Apr. 1930. 839.00/3370.

[37]*Ibid.*

[38]Curtis to Cotton. 21 Apr. 1930. 839.00/3383.

In the meantime, the opposition to Trujillo had forged the coalition that Curtis had predicted. The Progresistas and the Partido Nacional put their differences aside and nominated Velásquez for the presidency and Angel Morales for the vice-presidency. They approached the election without enthusiasm, however. On April 26, W.A. Bickers, the American Consul at Puerto Plata, reported that the members of the Alianza--the name given to the coalition--had nearly ceased campaigning. The party leaders and workers thought it hardly worth it to risk their lives working against Trujillo when their chances for victory were nonexistent.[39]

Curtis confirmed this report and, by May 15, could inform the Department that the Alianza had withdrawn from the election and had urged the voters not to go to the polls. This was, and is, a measure commonly practiced in Latin American political campaigns and is intended to cast doubt on the validity of the election.[40] It is a tactic of doubtful utility on all occasions but was particularly ineffective in this instance. Trujillo could not have been concerned less with the lack of participation in the election by his opponents. When the votes had been counted Trujillo showed a total of 223,000 in his favor, greatly in excess, Curtis observed, of the total number of registered voters in the Republic.[41]

---

[39] W.A. Bickers to Cotton. 26 Apr. 1930. 839.00/3390.

[40] Curtis to Cotton. 15 May 1930. 839.00/3404.

[41] <u>For. Rel.</u> II. 1930. Curtis to Cotton. 19 May 1930. 839.00 Elections/13. p. 723.

All of Curtis' condemnations of Trujillo did not bring about a change in the attitude of the Department of State. It adhered to the policy of non-involvement established at the outset and evinced no interest in any of the reports of fraud and violence perpetrated on behalf of Trujillo's candidacy. On one of Curtis' dispatches describing some of these events, Cotton attached a note asking Dana G. Munro for his views on the matter. Munro replied wearily, "Events like this are not uncommon in Caribbean elections."[42] There is nothing startling or incisive in this remark, but it is indicative of the Department's passive attitude toward the course of events in the Dominican Republic.

It has already been shown that the State Department was determined to recognize Trujillo or anyone else who came to power as a result of the elections. As the nature of the campaign became known through Curtis' dispatches, this intention was carried a step further. In a departmental memo to Munro on April 11, 1930, Francis White, Assistant Secretary of State, wrote that it was presumed that, ". . . the intention would be to recognize Trujillo even were the elections palpably fraudulent or the result due to intimidation by the military forces."[43]

The only interpretation that can be given to this statement is that the Department intended to recognize Trujillo even if he acquired the presidency by ensuring the results of the

---

[42]Munro memo to Cotton, attached to Curtis dispatch to Cotton. 5 Apr. 1930. 839.00/3366.

[43]White memo to Munro. 11 Apr. 1930. 839.00/3394.

election with the use of force. This came very close to saying that he would be recognized even if he seized the presidency by force. There is little reason to doubt that this is precisely what it meant. Evidence of this is seen in a letter from Cotton to Ray Lyman Wilbur, Secretary of the Interior. Cotton explained that the only alternative to letting Trujillo have the presidency by any means he might wish to use was the sending in of the marines. This, Cotton wrote, he was unwilling to consider except as a very last resort.[44]

As a "last resort" to what, Cotton did not explain. Presumably he had in mind potential danger to American lives and property or interference with the collection of customs. It is clear that he did not mean marines would be sent, as a "last resort," to prevent Trujillo from becoming president. He had already ruled out any other alternative as a means to that end. He had, therefore, arrived, at the "very last resort" and was unwilling to consider it. It has already been shown that nonrecognition would not be used to prevent Trujillo from seizing the presidency. It is highly unlikely, therefore, that the more extreme measure of sending in the marines would be used for that purpose. It is significant, nevertheless, that intervention was reserved as a possible alternative for whatever eventuality Cotton had in mind. It is indicative once again of the reservations in the policy of the Hoover administration regarding

[44]Letter from Joseph P. Cotton, Undersecretary of State, to Ray Lyman Wilbur, Secretary of the Interior. 839.00/3397.

non-intervention.

The reason for adhering strictly to a policy of non-involvement was stated clearly by Francis White in the memo to Munro referred to above. He wrote that the Department wished to avoid entirely the possibility that the policy of the United States would seem to have the effect of intervening or interfering in any way whatever in Dominican domestic affairs. He was aware, however, of the dilemma challenging the policy of the United States pointed to by Curtis. White questioned whether the American image in the Dominican Republic or in Latin America generally would be enhanced ". . . if we are to allow Trujillo to establish himself by force or anything bordering on a coup d'état."[45]

Trujillo saved the Department any agony it might have had to endure in such an event by observing the formality of an election. On the other hand, technical observation of a constitutional procedure by Trujillo did not free the United States of the charge of complicity in his rise to power. It was and still is a popular pastime in certain South and North American quarters to berate the United States for not having taken steps to prevent him from seizing the Dominican presidency. It did not, the argument goes, because Trujillo was an avowed friend of American policies and American economic interests received favorable treatment during his regime.

This point of view simply does not stand up under even a cursory examination of the evidence. It is made clear over and

---

[45]White memo to Munro, 11 Apr. 1930, 839.00/3394.

again in State Department communications that the United States did not wish to risk the damage to its goodwill in Latin America that interference in the Dominican election would bring. Its established policy from beginning to end in the Dominican presidential campaign was to recognize the government of whoever won the election. Moreover, it did attempt to discourage Trujillo from seeking the office. Admittedly, the State Department recognized the futility of this effort. It was as far as it felt it could go, however, without incurring the charge of interference.

The assertion that the United States positively favored Trujillo can be refuted on other grounds as well. In the first place it assumes that the United States deliberately designed the situation that provided Trujillo with his opportunity. Quite the contrary is true, of course. All of the efforts by the United States and its representatives in Santo Domingo before and during the revolution were designed to promote the stability of Dominican political institutions. Aside from this Curtis bent every effort to exclude Trujillo from the presidency during the Negotiations terminating the revolution.

The contention that the United States favored Trujillo because his regime would benefit American financial interests is equally untenable. Before Hoover left office, Trujillo would on more than one occasion prove that his reputation in this respect was highly overrated. Furthermore, none of the candidates in the Dominican election of 1930 presented any threat to American economic interests. The candidates of the Alianza, Velásquez and Morales, were known quantities and probably were preferable from the standpoint of economic interests.

Another critic of Hoover's Dominican policy takes a different slant. Albert C. Hicks, an American journalist, has charged that the "recognition of the Trujillo Government from the start was most certainly one of the stupidities of mankind."[46] The only explanation that he could find for it was in the "utter negligence" of an administration that regarded the problems of the Dominican Republic as too small for its serious attention in the face of the international economic crisis.[47] It is true, of course, that international financial conditions, in part at least, had prevented the United States from resisting effectively Trujillo's rise to power. Negligence, however, is not the proper term to describe this situation. Even had the Hoover administration thought it desirable to openly oppose Trujillo, it is an inescapable fact that because of the international depression, the United States was limited in how far it could extend itself in Latin America. This was not negligence but a condition not within the power of the United States to control.

Hicks' study was also written from the vantage point of 1946. He was indignant--even angry--that Trujillo had been able to impose his cruel dictatorship on the Dominican people for so long without incurring the censure of the United States. It had been recognized in 1930, of course, that Trujillo's regime would

---

[46]Albert C. Hicks. Blood in the Streets. (New York, 1946) p. 92.

[47]Ibid. p. 88.

be a dictatorship. It could not have been foreseen, however, just how vicious and enduring that regime would be.

No criticism of United States policy, whether valid or hackneyed, can escape an essential truth. The Dominicans, at least those of education and affluence, were responsible for their own plight. Their leaders had made a game of betraying each other and every principle they had ever pronounced. No pledge made was too sacred to be broken if it stood in the way of place, power, and peculation. Perhaps Colonel Cutts was correct when he wrote that wealth procured through control of the government was "what they all want."[48] His error was in excluding Trujillo from those motivated by this consideration.

[48]Cutts report from Port au Prince, enclosed in White dispatch to Cabot, 18 Jan. 1930. 839.00/3341.

CHAPTER VI

THE DOMINICAN FINANCIAL CRISIS AND LOAN NEGOTIATIONS OF 1930

The resolution of the Dominican political situation removed one of the serious problems with which the United States was faced in its relations with the Republic. A new problem, equally vexing and extending over a longer period of time, followed quickly on the heels of the "election" of Trujillo. Dominican finances, like those of every other Latin American country, had been falling into an increasingly desperate state since the onset of the international depression. The revolution of February had given impetus to the forces creating this condition and the United States, owing to its prerogatives stipulated in the Customs Convention of 1924, became intimately involved in Dominican efforts to solve its financial problems.

The prosperity of the Dominican economy depended upon the export of its major agricultural products, sugar, coffee and cacao. The sharp decline in the price of these commodities resulted in a decrease of income and, therefore, the purchasing power of Dominicans. Since the Dominican government relied upon sales and excise taxes as the most important source of its internal revenues, the inability and unwillingness of the consumer to buy resulted in a drastic decline in government income.[1]

The lack of purchasing power also caused a sharp decline in imports resulting in a steady reduction in customs receipts.

---

[1]Memorandum by Winthrop R. Scott to Cotton. 24 Apr. 1930. 839.51/3206.

When deductions were made for the service of the bonded indebtedness little remained for remittance to the Dominican goverment. Compounding these difficulties was the fact that in 1930 the first payments on the principal of the bond issues of 1922 and 1926 were due. Only payment of the interest, amounting to $1,100,000 annually, had been required before March 20, 1930. Amortization payments totaling $1,800,000 annually had to be remitted to the fiscal agent of the loan after that date.[2]

The service charges, amounting to a combined total of $2,900,000 annually, when deducted from a source of revenue already in a state of decline, resulted in a sharply reduced income for a hard pressed Dominican government. Ultimately, revenues derived from customs were insufficient even to meet the full service of the interest and amortization on the outstanding bonds. It will be recalled that the Convention of 1924 had provided that one-twelfth of the annual service charges were to be remitted each month. This meant that approximately $240,000 was needed each month to meet these charges. By September, 1931, customs receipts fell $63,000 short of this amount.[3] The following month the deficiency amounted to $77,000.[4]

The Dominican government was in obvious need of relief from

---

[2]Edwin C. Wilson to Cordell Hull. 22 Mar. 1933. 839.51/3896.

[3]M.L. Stafford, American charge at Santo Domingo, to Stimson. 14. Sept. 1931. 839.51/3487.

[4]<u>For. Rel.</u> II. 1931. H.F. Arthur Schoenfeld, American Minister to the Dominican Republic, to Stimson. 20 Oct. 1931. 839.51/3542. p. 124.

these pressing conditions. It first attempted to alleviate the strain on its finances by negotiating a refunding loan of first, fifty, and then, twenty-five million dollars. Failing in this, it then sought temporary relief through a smaller loan of $5,000,000. When this too ended in failure, Trujillo declared a moratorium on the payments of the principal, but not the interest, of the bond issues of 1922 and 1926. An examination of the response to these developments by the United States will reveal a policy that was sensitive to the opinion of the hemisphere but also careful to preserve presumed American rights.

That the Dominican financial situation was becoming desperate had been apparent even before Trujillo was elected in May, 1930. Henry P. Seidemann and T.D. Addison of the Brookings Institute had surveyed the prevailing economic conditions in April of that year. They revealed their findings to Winthrop R. Scott of the Latin American Division who relayed them to Cotton.

Seidemann and Addison confirmed the suspicion already widely held that the Dominican economy was suffering from a sharp decline in personal and public income. The uncertain political conditions then obtaining merely aggravated what was already a chaotic financial situation. They saw little reason to hope for a rapid recovery.[5] The Department was supplied with additional information in this regard by Cabot on April 30. He reported that exports had fallen off drastically and imports were decreasing apace.[6]

---

[5]Scott memo to Cotton. 24 Apr. 1930. 839.51/3206.

[6]Cabot report on economic conditons. Enclosed in: Curtis to Stimson. 30 Apr. 1930. 839.51/3207.

The consequences of these impersonal forces were not the only ones disrupting the Dominican economy. Fiscal mismanagement and widespread corruption in public office had accelerated the financial collapse of the country. Seidemann and Addison had reported that Trujillo was extremely unpopular among the "responsible elements" in the Republic. In part, this was the result of what these considered to be his low birth and because he led a dissolute personal life. They were opposed to him also because it was known that while Commander of the army he had accumulated a fortune through graft. Neither did they regard Trujillo as competent to deal with the financial crisis.[7]

Curtis confirmed this view sometime later. In May of 1931, he observed that one of Trujillo's greatest obstacles to efficient administration was that educated and responsible Dominicans refused to serve in his government. They were, of course, opposed to his dictatorial methods and the corruption of his regime. They refused to associate with him on social occasions as well. As a result, Trujillo had to rely upon unsavory as well as incompetent aids to conduct the business of government.[8]

If competency in administration was in short supply, honesty was absent altogether. Cabot had reported that Estrella had expressed a sincere interest in economizing in administration and in weeding out incompetents. Clearly, the elimination of some jobs and the embezzlement of public funds by office holders

---

[7]Scott memo to Cotton. 24 Apr. 1930. 839.51/3206.

[8]Curtis to Stimson. 29 May 1931. 839.00/3490.

and their relatives and friends could result in great savings. He observed, however, that this would be contrary ". . . to the practices of every Dominican administration which has ever come to power." In practice, Cabot concluded, the Estrella government had followed the example of previous administrations in ". . . letting the morrow take care of itself; and . . . it will probably find the bottom of its forthcoming catastrophic financial fall paved with its good intentions."[9]

Three days later, May 3, 1930, Curtis affirmed that a wide gulf separated the expressed intentions and the practices of Estrella's administration. Superfluous jobs that had been eliminated upon the success of the revolution had been recreated and filled with supporters of the government. Moreover, officials were using their offices to line their own pockets and the national treasury was being used as a campaign chest for the forthcoming elections. These practices were adding to a deficit already amounting to $3,000,000.[10]

Two weeks later Curtis had received information from the manager of the Santo Domingo branch of the National City Bank of New York that wholesale embezzlement of government funds had been going on since the revolution and were being used primarily to finance the election campaign of General Trujillo. The frauds were increasing the deficit which would have been large even in

---

[9]Cabot report in: Curtis to Stimson. 30 Apr. 1930. 839.51/3207.

[10]Curtis to Stimson. 3 May 1930. 839.00 General Conditions/52.

the absence of criminal activities.[11]

Trujillo--who was the real executive power in the Republic although not inaugurated until August 1, 1930--attempted in two small ways to increase government revenues before turning to the United States for aid. First, he had his rubber stamp congress enact a law imposing a surcharge on certain imported luxury items. This was in fact a customs impost but proceeds derived therefrom would not be subject to deductions for servicing the foreign debt. This was an evasion, if not a direct violation, of the Convention of 1924. No protest was filed, however, and even Curtis was unusually quiet about it. The State Department did not expect that it would be an effective means of raising revenue because of graft in its collection.[12]

Trujillo, however, meant to avoid that pitfall in this instance--whether to enable the government to pay some of its bills or to make certain that the proceeds got as far as his own pocket is problematical. In either case, Trujillo requested, through a Marine Corps crony, Major Thomas E. Watson, that the duty be collected by the customs receivership.[13] It was typical of Trujillo that he requested the United States to collect for him a tax, the imposition of which was a violation, at least in spirit, of a treaty relationship with that country.

---

[11]Curtis to Stimson. 17 May 1930. 839.51/3218.

[12]Scott memo to Munro. 9 June 1930. 839.151/69.

[13]Curtis to Stimson. 6 June 1930. 839.51/3222.

The matter was allowed to rest until after Trujillo's inauguration. On September 12, 1930, he proposed not only that the receivership collect the duties arising out of Law 190, but that it undertake to collect all of the Republic's internal revenues. The State Department had so far declined to permit the receivership to collect even the imposts on imported luxuries. As to this latest proposal both the Department and William E. Pulliam, the Receiver General of Dominican Customs, were agreed that a great deal more consideration of the matter was necessary before it could be approved. It left the matter of collection of the proceeds resulting from Law 190 to the discretion of Curtis.[14] Curtis had previously urged approval of this measure and on September 13, he authorized the receivership to undertake this task on a temporary basis.[15] In his reply acknowledging approval of this step, Cotton emphasized that it was ". . . definitely an emergency measure."[16]

The collection of this tax, regardless of how efficiently administered, could not have greatly increased the revenues of the Dominican government. Trujillo, even before this matter was resolved, resorted to a tried and true method of increasing the government's income--the issuance of government bonds for payment of daily operating costs. This floating debt became more

---

[14]Secretary of War Hurley to Stimson. 12 Sept. 1930. 839.51/3263.

[15]Curtis to Stimson. 13 Sept. 1930. 839.51/3264.

[16]Cotton to Curtis. 15 Sept. 1930. 839.51/3264.

or less permanent because the government was unable and unwilling to redeem it and it amounted to an increase in the public debt of the Republic in violation of the Convention of 1924. Curtis complained of this to the Department and asked that he be instructed to make a formal protest to the Dominican government.[17]

While the increase of the floating debt would become a serious concern to the State Department in 1931 and 1932, it did not at this time see what, if anything, could be accomplished by an official protest. Attached to Curtis' dispatch were memoranda initialed by Scott and Munro expressing the view that no instructions concerning this matter were required.[18]

On June 18, 1930, Cabot took up Curtis' line and urged the Department to take some action protesting the repeated violations of the Convention. In an effort to impress upon the Department of State the need to restrict the increase of the Dominican public debt in further violation of the Convention, he forwarded a report compiled by the Dominican government describing its financial condition in the most optimistic terms possible. Even so, Cabot pointed out that the deficit for 1930 would be $2,000,000. Cabot suggested that this report ". . . be used as a basis for any diplomatic action which the Department may feel disposed to take in order to prevent the further accumulation of this deficit."[19] In closing his report, Cabot remarked:

17Curtis to Stimson. 30 Apr. 1930. 839.51/3207.

18*Ibid*. Memoranda by Scott and Munro.

19Cabot to Stimson. 18 June 1930. 839.51/3227.

> While there are certain responsibilities which the United States obviously should avoid, if only from the point of view of our relations with other Latin American countries, at the same time it appears of great importance that the evident and serious violation of the Treaty obligations of this country to the United States should not be ignored.[20]

In a memorandum attached to this document, Scott noted that he had discussed this matter with Munro some weeks before and it had been agreed that the United States should not initiate any action. He stated clearly the reasons for assuming this attitude. Scott wrote:

> As matters now stand, although the Dominicans are having a hard time, they are still meeting the service of the foreign debt, including the very heavy amortization charges, and as long as they are able to do this it would not appear desirable for the Department to take any steps to change the present status.[21]

From the point of view of the United States this was an eminently reasonable position to take. As long as the interests of American holders of Dominican bonds were not affected, the State Department had little about which to complain given existing economic conditions. The Dominican government was hard pressed financially with or without corruption and maladministration and it was essential that it raise funds in one way or another. It should have been obvious to Curtis that no number of protests by the United States against the means by which this was accomplished would increase Dominican revenues. Irrespective of any repercussions that official protests, or some stronger action,

---

[20]Ibid.

[21]Ibid. Scott memo to Walter C. Thurston.

may have had throughout Latin America, such a step simply would not have alleviated the condition bringing it about in the first place.

The State Department was not unmindful, however, of the likelihood that the Dominican government could not ensure indefinitely the payment of the debt service. Imports continued their steady decline and monthly customs receipts were already, in the summer of 1930, falling dangerously close to the minimum amount needed for the debt service. By September of 1930 they had fallen slightly short of the necessary sum but the deficit was made up with October's receipts.[22] This meant, of course, that the Dominican government was realizing practically no revenue from customs at a time when it was badly in need of some new resource. It was recognized in the State Department that a more far-reaching solution was needed for the Dominican government than the small efforts so far made by Trujillo. At the same time, however, it had been decided that the proposed means for such a solution would have to come from the Dominicans. Scott had written to Walter C. Thurston of the Latin American Affairs Division that he and Munro had discussed the matter and had agreed ". . . that it would be better for the Dominican Government to initiate any action which might be considered in regard to the financial situation."[23]

---

[22]Secretary of War Hurley to Stimson. 6 Sept. 1930. 839.51/3256.

[23]Scott memo to Thurston. Enclosed in: Cabot to Stimson. 18 June 1930. 839.51/3227.

Trujillo did not keep the State Department waiting long for his proposals. On June 5, 1930, he approached Curtis on the subject of floating a new loan in the United States and tentatively suggested that it be in the form of a refunding operation of one of the earlier bond issues. This would have the effect of moving back the due date for amortization thus releasing a greater share of the revenue derived from customs to the Dominican government. He wanted the loan to be large enough, however, to provide some ready cash for public works projects. Curtis advised him that such a loan could be obtained only if secured by the customs receipts which in turn would require an extension of the receivership. Trujillo replied that he understood this and that he regarded the receivership as beneficial to his country and was prepared to see its life prolonged.[24]

When informed of Trujillo's proposition, Scott saw two major difficulties. First, owing to the conditions of the market and of the state of the Dominican economy, he foresaw great difficulty in interesting bankers in the loan. Secondly, if such a loan proposal were to be approved by the Department, ". . . it would be essential that the entire public works program be determined in advance, as otherwise money budgeted for that purpose would be improperly diverted."[25]

Trujillo was persistent, however, and again broached the subject of a loan with Curtis. He opened this discussion with a

---

[24]Curtis to Stimson. 5 June 1930. 839.51/3220.

[25]Scott memo to Munro. 9 June 1930. 839.151/69.

frank appraisal of the Dominican financial situation and the dire need of funds by the government. He then remarked that it was his intention to consult Curtis at all times and to be guided by his advice.[26] This was a strange sentiment coming from Trujillo who had earlier taken pains to inform the State Department of his dislike for Curtis and had complained frequently of the latter's inclination not to recognize his government after he was elected.[27] Moreover, because of his views, which were well known, Curtis had received discourteous treatment from Dominican government officials.[28]

During the Dominican election campaign Munro, determined to strengthen Curtis' hand, had advised that it be made clear to the new Dominican Minister, Rafael Brache, that the Department was ". . . being guided entirely by Curtis' recommendation . . ." in its Dominican policy.[29] That this advice was followed became apparent a short time later when Brache questioned Scott about the position the United States would assume when Trujillo was elected. It had been rumored, he complained, that the United States would not recognize his government because of Curtis' attitude. Scott replied merely that the matter was then under

---

[26]Curtis to Stimson. 6 June 1930. 839.51/3222.

[27]Scott memo of conversation with Rafael Brache, Dominican Minister to the United States. 12 May 1930. 839.00/3430. See also: Scott memoranda of 8 Apr. 1930. 839.00 Presidential Campaigns/17; and 1 July 1930. 839.001 Trujillo, Rafael 1./2.

[28]Thurston memo to Harvey H. Bundy, Undersecretary of State. 19 Aug. 1931. 839.51/3543.

[29]Munro memo to Cotton. 9 Apr. 1930. 839.00 Presidential Campaigns/16.

advisement.[30] It will be recalled that in fact it had already been decided that Trujillo would be recognized even if his election was "palpably fraudulent."

Under these circumstances Trujillo, in his hope for approval of a loan, had decided to mend his fences, albeit temporarily, with Curtis.[31] Curtis was not taken in. In his reply to the Department he remarked that Trujillo had consulted him only because he was in need of money. Curtis doubted if Trujillo would really be guided by his advice. He added, ". . . not having respected his word in the past, he must prove its value in the future by his actions."[32] Curtis was inclined, nevertheless, to give favorable consideration to the request for a loan. Trujillo, he wrote, ". . . through his control of the army . . . dominates the country which means that he can, if he chooses, do more for its good or harm than lies within the power of anyone else."[33] In this remark Curtis struck close to a theme to become of increasing importance in the relations of the United States with Trujillo. In the final resolution of the Dominican financial crisis he came to represent the only alternative, however

---

[30]Scott memo of conversation with Brache. 21 Apr. 1930. 839.00 Presidential Campaigns/19.

[31]It was temporary because he never really forgave Curtis. In August, 1931, he was considering having Curtis declared persona non grata. Curtis was, in the meantime, removed from his post. After he had left he received abusive treatment in the Trujillo controlled press. (Thurston memo to Bundy. 19 Aug. 1931. 839.51/3543).

[32]Curtis to Stimson. 6 June 1930. 839.51/3222.

[33]*Ibid.*

distasteful, to chaos.

Trujillo's efforts to negotiate a loan went very slowly during the summer of 1930. The State Department was offering little encouragement and Trujillo was somewhat hesitant to present any concrete and detailed proposal of his own. A natural disaster intruded upon the scene, however, to give Trujillo an opening wedge for negotiations. A devastating hurricane struck Santo Domingo on September 4, destroying, according to an estimate by Curtis, ninety-nine percent of the city and its environs.[34] This was probably somewhat high but it indicates that the hurricane was exceptionally violent.

The Trujillo government sent a panicky telegram to its Legation in Washington.

> Situation appalling . . . eight hundred bodies have been recovered and an immense number injured . . . . Lack of food is being felt. Families without clothing. Medical supplies insufficient . . . . It is urgent to communicate this to the American Government; . . . to the American Press, to the Red Cross and the noble American people.[35]

What may have been the most sincere communication in the long life of the Trujillo dictatorship ended on an opportunistic note, however. The instruction concluded: "Act quickly . . . sound out the State Department as to their feeling as to the possible necessity of a loan."[36]

---

[34]For. Rel. II. 1930. Curtis to Stimson. 4 Sept. 1930 836.48 1930 Hurricane/1.

[35]Ibid. Dominican Government to its Washington Legation. 4 Sept. 1930. 836.48 1930 Hurricane/23. pp. 727-728.

[36]Ibid. p. 728.

The United States responded by sending a commissioner, Eliot Wadsworth, to the Republic to investigate its financial needs. Wadsworth, who did not speak Spanish and was uninformed on Dominican political affairs, added little to the knowledge already possessed by the Department of State concerning the country he was to visit. He remained only one week and ". . . painted the situation in markedly darker colors than was warranted."[37]

Wadsworth seems to have been taken in by Trujillo. In his report of his mission he placed great emphasis on the Dominican budget, a completely meaningless document, and as an analysis of the Dominican economy his report was largely useless. His recommendations, however, were all that Trujillo could have asked for. Wadsworth proposed that amortization payments be suspended for two years and, to maintain the solvency of the Dominican government, that a loan be approved providing it with a cash balance.[38]

The subject of a moratorium, or suspension of payments, had come up before but Trujillo, anxious to get approval of a loan, had rejected the idea. In an appeal to what he considered to be the deep rooted instincts of the State Department, he declared it to be his "firmest intention" to meet the full service of the debt, ". . . whatever may be the obstacles." Trujillo continued,

---

[37]Stafford to Stimson. 710G/41.

[38]Wadsworth Report. 13 Oct. 1930. FW 839.51 Wadsworth Mission/13.

> I can make this emphatic declaration because, aside from my own energetic will, . . . I know, above all, the high concept which the Dominican people hold, that the exact fulfillment of our international obligations constitutes the most solid basis for hoping to see prompt and real reconstruction.[39]

Trujillo not only wished to enhance his reputation with the State Department but also with American businessmen. The note containing the above statements ended with this instruction to the Dominican Minister: "Please communicate these statements to the Department of State and make them known to the American Press."[40]

Perhaps Trujillo knew what he was about. The combination of Rooseveltian braggadocio and invocation of American homespun had the desired effect, temporarily at least. Stimson was as much taken with Trujillo as Wadsworth had been. He confided to his diary that the general ". . . is panning out to be a very good man."[41] Stimson not only favored the idea of suspending amortization payments but believed that Trujillo was just the man to spend money diverted from the sinking fund to reconstruct the country and keep it out of the hands of the "vultures" and "politicoes" who would want to ". . . reap a rich harvest of graft."[42] In due course, Stimson would change his mind about Trujillo and would come to view the suspension of amortization payments to the sinking fund as a more complicated business than

---

[39]A note from the Dominican Government to the State Department. 10 Sept. 1930. 839.51/3265.

[40]<u>Ibid</u>.

[41]Stimson. <u>Diaries</u>. X. 13 Oct. 1930. p. 64.

[42]<u>Ibid</u>. p. 65.

at first it appeared.

Meanwhile, Trujillo was prepared to forego a moratorium because his plan for a loan was on the grand scale. Soon after Wadsworth had completed his mission Trujillo appointed a Commission to go to the United States to negotiate with the Department of State and American bankers the means by which the Dominican financial crisis could be resolved. Appointed for this task were Elias Brache, Foreign Minister, Rafael Brache, his brother and Minister to the United States, and Roberto Despradel who had served as a contact man for Trujillo with the rebels before the February revolution. Other than this, and that they were seeking a loan, Curtis, in his dispatch to the Department concerning the appointments to the Commission, reported that he had been unable to learn very much about the Commission or the details of its plan. When the Department replied that it had not been in contact with the Commission Curtis went to Trujillo to learn what he could of its progress.[43]

Curtis discovered, however, that Trujillo claimed to be as much in the dark as he was. The dictator told Curtis that he had received only one report, and that unsatisfactory, from the Commissioners. Furthermore, Trujillo complained, they had deviated from their instructions when they had not gone first to the Department of State to explain their purposes. He then remarked that he had sent Rafael Vidal to the United States to discover

---

[43]Stimson to Curtis. 11 Nov. 1930. 839.51/3289.

what the Commissioners were up to but he did not reveal to Curtis what their original instructions had been.[44]

Curtis received some information about the purpose of the Dominican Economic Commission from an American whose name he did not reveal. The project that the Commissioners had in mind, Curtis was told, involved the organization of a government monopoly on all public utilities. The management of this monopoly, and one on tobacco and "other agricultural products," would be assigned to bankers who would provide the funds for establishing the monopolies. Trujillo had apparently reached no final decision in the matter but had held up negotiations on the sale of the government owned telephone system to an interested American firm because this was included in the public utility monopoly under consideration.[45]

The representative of the American firm interested in the purchase of the telephone system was the same unnamed American relating these facts to Curtis. He went on to say that Abelardo R. Nanita, first official biographer of Trujillo, and Trujillo's notoriously dissolute uncle, Pina Chevalier, had been appointed to a Commission to study this project and had long ago reported favorably upon it. The scheme had apparently originated with Rafael Brache and Curtis' source claimed that he had heard Brache hint and Nanita openly avow that, ". . . there would be splendid opportunities for them, and probably also for the American, to

---

[44]*Ibid*.

[45]Curtis Stimson. 24 Nov. 1930. 839.51/3300.

make some money if the project should be adopted by the government."[46] Curtis reported that it appeared to him very likely that Rafael Brache had persuaded the Commission to base their efforts to acquire a loan on this project.[47]

Trujillo may have been, as he claimed, uninformed of the activities of his Commissioners. He could hardly have been surprised, however, in light of Curtis' revelations concerning the utilities monopoly, that they had not gone to the State Department as a first step in accomplishing these purposes. The State Department was not prepared to accept the verdict that Trujillo was himself deeply involved in this scheme. It had learned from other sources something of the nature of the monopoly scheme and Thurston wrote that Curtis' report was "substantially accurate." He blamed the Brache brothers, however, and not Trujillo for the financial chicanery being promoted.[48]

The reasons for restraint in condemning Trujillo for whatever part he may have had in the scheme is found in the growing conviction among Department personnel that he was the only one in sight able to govern the Republic. On November 14, Francis White had written that, in a meeting between himself, Cotton, Wadsworth and David Hunter Miller of the historical office, it had been concluded that there was no one in sight at that time who could

---

[46]Ibid.

[47]Ibid.

[48]Thurston memo to Scott. 4 Dec. 1930. 839.51 Economic Mission/1 1/2.

replace Trujillo. It might, therefore, be worthwhile to help him out of his financial difficulties. White explained that there had been no endorsement of Trujillo, but a recognition that he was there to stay. The only alternative to him seemed to be chaos.[49] In consideration of such an attitude it was to be expected that there would be reluctance to paint him any darker than necessary.

Little else seems to have been learned of the Dominican Commission's meanderings until they arrived in Washington to present their plan to the Department of State. The project submitted for approval was quite extraordinary in view of the international economic conditions then obtaining. The Dominican Commissioners proposed that a loan be approved for $50,000,000 at 5 1/2 per cent to be redeemed in forty years and secured by Dominican Customs under the receivership arrangement. Twenty million dollars of this amount would be used to refund the bond issues of 1922 and 1926. Aside from this, $3,000,000 was to be provided for loans to property owners in Santo Domingo to rebuild facilities destroyed by the hurricane; $3,000,000 for the capitalization of a bank for agricultural loans; $7,000,000 was needed for the capitalization of a Formento, or Development, Corporation to be operated jointly by the government and private business (this was the monopoly scheme reported by Curtis);

---

[49]White memo of conversation between himself, Undersecretary Cotton, Wadsworth and David Hunter Miller, 4 Dec. 1930. 839.51 Wadsworth Mission/19.

$9,000,000 for a public works program and $3,000,000 for the purchase by the Dominican government of the tobacco, alcohol and explosives industries.[50] This left $5,000,000 unaccounted for. Presumably it would be used for the retirement of the deficit incurred since January, 1930. No mention was made of it, however.

On January 3, 1931, Rafael Brache visited the Department and in an interview with Thurston urged that he give the Commissioners some encouraging word to take to New York bankers in order to accelerate negotiations. In defense of the plan he said that if approved it would enable the Dominican Republic to continue to purchase all of its wheat and petroleum from the United States. Then, rather desperately, he threatened that if approval were not granted, the Republic might be forced to purchase wheat from Canada and oil from Dutch Shell rather than from producers in the United States. He also warned that if American bankers did not support the plan it was very likely that Canadian bankers would. On the memorandum giving an account of this interview was a marginal note, uninitialed but probably written by Thurston, pointing out that even if Canadian bankers were so inclined the plan still required the approval of the United States according to the terms of the Convention of 1924.[51]

All that Thurston said to Brache was that the matter had been

---

[50]Memorial presented to President Hoover by the Dominican Economic Commission. 31 Dec. 1930. 839.51 Economic Mission/5.

[51]Thurston memo of conversation with Rafael Brache. 3 Jan. 1931. 839.51 Economic Mission/6.

taken under advisement.[52] The State Department was not long in reaching a decision, however. On January 9, Cotton advised that the Dominican Commissioners be told quite candidly, ". . . that their plan for a $50,000,000 loan is impossible; that the plan has not the consent of the American Government."[53] In less straightforward language, this is what they were told the next day. It was pointed out to the Commissioners that, while the United States was interested in helping them in their difficulty, they were not doing their country any favor by encumbering it with a debt for forty years.[54] They were told also that there was little possibility that a loan of the amount proposed could be floated under the market conditions then prevailing.[55]

A smaller loan, however, had not been ruled out. At the same time that he had advised a flat rejection of the $50,000,000 loan scheme, Cotton had recommended that the Dominicans be told to study proposals for a small loan--about $5,000,000--that might "hold the situation" for a year of so.[56] This recommendation was not in accord with the policy established by the Department relative to small loans during the last months of 1930.

---

[52]Ibid.

[53]Cotton memo to Stimson. 9 Jan. 1931. 839.51 Economic Mission/10.

[54]Memo of conversation between the Dominican Commissioners and Cotton, White, Scott and Miller. 10 Jan. 1931. 839.51 Economic Mission/12.

[55]Curtis to Stimson. 12 Jan. 1931. 839.51 Economic Mission/8.

[56]Cotton to Stimson. 9 Jan. 1931. 839.51 Economic Mission/10.

Negotiations for a smaller loan had been undertaken during the weeks following the hurricane of September 4, with two firm proposals the result. One loan proposal came from Ulen and Company, a construction firm, which was rejected by the Department of State. It gave as reasons, that, first, no decision had yet been reached to approve any kind of loan. Secondly, it had been learned that the proposal by Ulen and Company was tied to construction contracts in the Dominican Republic.[57] Thirdly, the proposal provided financing of a strictly temporary nature. The problem of Dominican finances would merely be adjourned for a year and at the end of 1931 would have to be met again.[58] Lee, Higginson and Company, a New York banking house and the fiscal agent for the bond issues of 1922 and 1926, had also proposed a loan for $5,000,000. Theirs too had been rejected in November because it provided only temporary relief.[59]

The encouragement that Cotton gave to the Dominican Commissioners to seek a smaller loan "to hold the situation" can only be viewed as a means of putting them off gently. A decision had been made by December of 1930 to oppose any new loan, large or small, to afford financial relief to the Dominican Republic. Stimson had been mildly favorable to a proposal by Lee, Higginson to refinance the Dominican debt brought to his attention on

---

[57] Miller memo to Cotton. 24 Nov. 1930. 839.51/3302.

[58] Cotton memo. 26 Nov. 1930. 839.51/3291 1/2.

[59] White memo of conversation with Cotton, Wadsworth and Miller. 14 Nov. 1930. 839.51 Wadsworth Mission/19.

November 14. At first glance, he saw it as ". . . a chance to get out of a very difficult situation."[60] In ten days of thinking it over, he changed his mind. On November 24, he told a visiting United States Senator that there was ". . . no chance on any bond issue at present . . ." for the Dominican Republic.[61] On the following day, in a conversation with William Borah, the subject of the security of loans to Latin America came up and Stimson, specifically mentioning the Dominican Republic, remarked that the United States ". . . was confronting the time when we would have to treat those countries in the way a court treats an insolvent corporation . . . ."[62]

What, precisely, Stimson meant by this dark suggestion is not altogether clear. He had been inspired to it first during a discussion of Dominican affairs with Cotton, White and Miller on November 11. Allowing that something had to be done about the Dominican financial crisis, he told them that

> We . . . must act somewhat along the line in which a court acts in the case of the insolvency of a corporation, and impound the assets and have them paid out virtually under our supervision. . . .[63]

Although Stimson instructed his aids to draft a specific course of action incorporating this idea, nothing ever came of it. It probably reflected Stimson's impatience more than a serious

---

[60]Stimson. Diaries. X. Nov. 14, 1930. p. 153.

[61]Ibid. Nov. 24, 1930. p. 175.

[62]Ibid. Nov. 25, 1930. p. 181.

[63]Ibid. Nov. 11, 1930. pp. 146-147.

intention to carry out its rather draconian implications. What is clear from the record is that no new loans to the Dominican Republic would be approved. Other means would have to be found to resolve that country's financial difficulties.

CHAPTER VII

THE DOMINICAN DEBT MORATORIUM OF 1931

The Dominican financial crisis had reached the critical point by the end of 1930. The customs receipts were no longer sufficient to meet the interest and amortization payments on the external debt. Internal revenues were insufficient to make up the difference. That some measure to bring relief had to be devised, and soon, was not in doubt. Refinancing the external debt via a new loan to accomplish this had been rejected. To allow Trujillo to default was unthinkable. The only recourse left was a moratorium. For a variety of reasons, a simple and direct route to this single, acceptable alternative was not available to the State Department. A serpentine course was plotted by which the Trujillo government would have to bear the onus of suspending payments to the sinking fund of the outstanding bonds, and the State Department could with a tarnished but still intact dignity shrug its shoulders to the irate bondholders clamoring for it to do its duty.

The first step was to obstruct the attempts being made by the Dominicans to obtain a new loan without appearing to do so. On January 26, Rafael Brache and Despradel held an interview with Francis White. The Dominicans recalled that Cotton had, on January 10, raised the possibility of a small short-term loan. Brache requested ". . . a definite authorization from the Department for a stipulated number of dollars . . ." that he could take to bankers in New York as a starting point for negotiations. White replied that this could not be done. The Dominicans would have to get a definite and detailed proposal and submit it to the Department for its consideration.[1] This position was entirely in accord with what had been the Department's standing policy since June, 1930, to leave the initiative to the Dominicans.[2]

The Dominicans, through Mr. Edward Gann, legal counsel for the Dominican Legation, submitted a plan to the Department on February 3, that received the personal attention of Secretary Stimson. The loan, arranged by the J. G. White Construction Company, was for the amount $5,000,000 at 5½ per cent interest to be redeemed over thirty years. Stimson expressed doubts about several features of the proposals. He first noted that bonds to raise the proceeds of the loan would sell at ninety cents on the dollar, that is, $4,500,000 would be realized from the sale of $5,000,000 in bonds. Stimson thought this "rather out of the ordinary" in light of market conditions and asked Gann if such a good bargain had not been accompanied by some understanding regarding

---

[1] For. Rel. II. 1931. White memo. 26 Jan. 1931. 839.51/3441 5/30. pp. 84-85.

[2] See above: Chapter VI. page 179. footnote 23.

construction contracts.[3] The Department had in its possession the contents of a letter from the Dominican Commissioners to J. G. White and Company authorizing it to negotiate a loan for them. The Commissioners stated that,

> In consideration of the services that you may render this Commission, the latter agrees to assist you in obtaining the engineering and construction work involved in our program, subject to mutually satisfactory contracts which you may enter into with the Dominican Government.[4]

This carefully worded arrangement was not careful enough to suppress suspicion concerning any loan between that company and the Dominican government. To Stimson's inquiry Gann replied, nevertheless, that it was a straight loan proposal unencumbered by prior agreements on construction contracts. He qualified his reply only to the extent of conceding that White and Company ". . . naturally hoped that they would be given preference on all public works to be undertaken in the future."[5]

Stimson was also concerned that no "commissions" would be paid to any person other than those ordinarily incurred in this type of an operation. He revealed that recently, in connection with a loan to an unspecified South American

---

[3]For. Rel. II. 1931. White memo of Gann interview with Stimson. 3 Feb. 1931. 839.51/3343. p. 86.

[4]Dominican Commission to the J. G. White Engineering Corporation. 20 Oct. 1930. 839.51/3261.

[5]For. Rel. II. 1931. White memo of Gann interview with Stimson. 3 Feb. 1931. 839.51/3343. p. 85.

country, a high government official had been paid such a "commission" and he asked Gann if anything of that nature were contemplated in the proposal under consideration. Gann replied that he had no knowledge of anything of this sort but agreed, at Stimson's behest, to "keep his eye peeled" for just such a thing.[6] Gann was not told that the Department's suspicion had been aroused by rumors then current and later confirmed that Trujillo had rejected a loan, similar to that arranged by White and Company, proposed by Ulen and Company because the latter had refused to pay a $50,000 bribe to high-ranking Dominican officials.[7]

Stimson did not keep the Dominicans waiting long for a reply. On February 12, he informed Rafael Brache that the proposed loan had been rejected. His stated reasons were that, first, the proposal "tied up" the Dominican government with an undefined obligation for an indefinite period with the White Company for the construction of public works projects. Secondly, no mention had been made in the loan contract of the amount the Dominican government would receive from the sale of the bonds. The bonds were to be sold at 90, but, Stimson observed, it was inconceivable under prevailing market conditions that the Dominican government could realize more than 78 on thirty year bonds. This, in Stimson's view, constituted "improvident borrowing." Thirdly, no provision

---

[6]Ibid. p. 86.

[7]Curtis to Stimson. 18 Aug. 1931. 839.51/3465.

had been made for the retirement of the Dominican floating debt. Furthermore, it did not provide any guarantee for the payment of the sinking fund charges for 1931, although this was ". . . not quite as strong a consideration . . . ."[8]

These were good and sufficient reasons for rejecting the proposal. They were not, however, the only or even the most important reasons. They do not answer the question why, if it wanted to eliminate financial chicanery in any loan proposal, the State Department did not take a hand in the negotiations. Any proposal submitted by the Dominicans would be suspect in that regard and was a standing reason for rejecting any loan presented for consideration. The State Department steadfastly declined, nevertheless, to participate in any negotiations. Moreover, it had been known all along that any proposed loan of whatever amount that the Dominicans might submit would of necessity have to be redeemed over a long period. It would be expensive and, therefore, constitute "improvident borrowing." Again, this amounted to a standing objection to any proposed loan.

The Department of State was fully aware that objections to a loan on the grounds that it did not provide for the retirement of the floating debt and a guarantee for amortization payments for one year were self-defeating.

---

[8] For. Rel. II. 1931. Scott memo of Brache interview with Stimson. 12 Feb. 1931. 839.51/3360. p. 88.

These two debts alone amounted to more than $4,000,000, as much of a cash return as could be realized by the Dominican government, owing to the conditions of the market, from a bond issue of $5,000,000. The Department of State had already registered objections to this kind of temporary financing because it would do nothing more than delay for a year or less the arrangement of a more permanent solution to the Dominican financial crisis.

The Dominicans were, nevertheless, encouraged to try again to negotiate a loan but his time with a reputable American banking house. Before another loan was considered, however, the Department, on February 12, forwarded to Curtis the general conditions that had to be met for the approval of any loan. These were five in number, of which four were a reiteration of stipulations already known. The first required that any proposal had to be submitted in complete and final form before it could be given consideration. The second stipulated that $5,000,000 should be the maximum amount borrowed at that time. The third stated that approval would not be given to any loan the terms of which amounted to "improvident borrowing." The fourth suggested that construction work in the Republic be limited to only the most necessary and desirable projects.[9]

The only new requirement, new at least for the Hoover administration, was the fifth. It stipulated that for any

---

[9] Ibid. Stimson to Curtis. 12 Feb. 1931. 839.51/3344a. pp. 90-91.

loan to be approved there would first have to be appointed an American financial adviser authorized to approve the disbursement of the proceeds of any loan.[10] The State Department had for so long shunned any proposal that would involve it so deeply in Dominican domestic affairs that this proposition coming at this time is extraordinary. It is possible, since it was well known that this was an unacceptable condition, that it was intended as the coup de grâce to any further Dominican efforts to float a new loan. On the other hand, the demand, whether or not it was ever imposed, would by itself incur the opprobium of the entire hemisphere, a risk that the United States had so far been unwilling to incur.

In light of this latter consideration, it is not surprising that the State Department retreated from this stipulation at the first opportunity. Curtis reported a few days later that Trujillo objected to this condition as "unduly mortifying" to Dominican national pride. He, Trujillo, suggested instead that the funds raised by a loan be deposited with Lee, Higginson and Company and that they honor the checks of the Dominican government only when accompanied by a duplicate signed by an American official designated by the State Department.[11] Without hesitation or qualification the

---

[10] Ibid. p. 90.

[11] Ibid. Curtis to Stimson. 5 Mar. 1931. 839.51/3366. pp. 92-93.

Department replied, on March 12, that it had no objection to this modification.[12]

In the meantime, on March 6, the Department had learned that Lee, Higginson was interested in considering a loan for four or five million dollars. As a basis for discussions, Lee, Higginson insisted on assurances that meaningful measures be undertaken to guarantee a program of economy and, in addition, that control of finances and expenditure of the proceeds of a loan be supervised by a representative of the State Department. It was suggested to Curtis that he recommend Lee, Higginson to Trujillo as the only firm that had evinced any interest in a Dominican loan.[13]

At the same time, however, nothing was said concerning the appointment by the State Department of a financial adviser. What Curtis was told was that the Department could recommend someone to Trujillo who it thought would fulfill the requirements stipulated by Lee, Higginson, but only if the Dominican president ". . . desired such an official . . . ." The individual whom the Department would recommend, if, and only if, it were asked to do so, was William E. Dunn.[14] This was a far cry from the demand for a financial adviser as stipulated

---

[12]Ibid. Stimson to Curtis. 12 Mar. 1931. 839.51/3367. p. 99.

[13]Ibid. Stimson to Curtis. 6 Mar. 1931. 839.51/3365. pp. 96-98.

[14]Ibid. p. 98.

on February 12. Dunn was not to be appointed by the State Department but instead by the Dominican government. In his reply Curtis wrote that Trujillo had requested that Dunn be sent immediately. He would receive a six month appointment ". . . with the possibility of increasing the period if a loan is obtained . . . ."[15]

Lee, Higginson, in the meantime, had drawn up a detailed preliminary plan for the flotation of a loan. The entire proposal, however, had been formulated upon the supposition that the State Department would appoint a financial adviser having all the powers necessary to control the expenditures of the Dominican government during the entire life of any new loan.[16]

The proposal had been sent to the Department on June 9, 1931. A few days later Francis White told W. McCormick Blair of Lee, Higginson, that the Department would not consider the proposal to appoint a financial adviser to the Dominican government. He told Blair that Lee, Higginson had apparently been misled by the arrangement between Dunn and the Dominican government. Dunn, White explained, was not an agent of the United States government. All that the Department had done was to suggest his name when asked to do so by Trujillo.

---

[15] _Ibid._ Curtis to Stimson. 9 Mar. 1931. 839.51/3367. p. 98.

[16] _Ibid._ Lee, Higginson and Company to White. 9 June 1931. 839.51/3415. p. 101.

Dunn was an agent of the Dominican government appointed at the pleasure of Trujillo. Blair rejoined testily that perhaps from then on his company should address their correspondence to Dunn and send only copies to the Department, the reverse of their previous practice. White replied merely that ". . . that was my view also and that we would be glad to be kept informed."[17]

That same day Lee, Higginson had been officially informed of the Department's disapproval of the financial adviser feature. The letter stated:

> The Department is not disposed to undertake any increased responsibilities vis-a-vis the finances of the Dominican Republic, beyond those set forth in the existing Convention . . . . Therefore the Department would not be disposed to be involved in the proposed arrangement for the Financial Adviser as set forth . . . (in) your letter of June ninth.[18]

With this discouraging news from the State Department, Lee, Higginson informed the Dominican government that it was no longer interested in proceeding with the negotiations.[19]

This was a complete about face from the attitude held by the Department as expressed in the instruction to Curtis on February 12. The only explanation is that the insistence

---

[17]White memo of telephone conversation with W. McCormick Blair. 30 June 1931. 839.51/3429.

[18]<u>For. Rel.</u> II. 1931. White letter to Lee, Higginson. 30 June 1931. 839.51/3428. pp. 106-107.

[19]<u>Ibid</u>. Lee, Higginson to White. 23 July 1931. 839.51/3448. p. 109.

upon acceptance of a financial adviser as a pre-condition for any loan had been intended to discourage the Dominicans from any further efforts. Before the Department had to press the issue, however, Lee, Higginson appeared on the scene, on March 6, proposing a loan requiring as one of its conditions the acceptance by the Dominican government of a financial adviser with sweeping powers to be appointed by the State Department. The Department quickly retreated from its previous position and stated that it would not become more deeply involved in Dominican finances by appointing a financial adviser. Thus, Lee, Higginson was left to reject the loan because its conditions had not been met. The State Department had climbed off its limb, had dexterously descended the trunk of the tree and had planted its feet firmly upon the ground.

Further support of the contention that the Department was opposed to any new loan and only wanted the Dominicans to come to their own conclusions is found in an exchange of views between Herbert Feis, Economic Adviser to the Department, and Dunn which took place on June 14. Feis told Dunn that, ". . . it was very doubtful if the Department could agree to any loan contract which would involve the extension of the life of the Convention beyond 1942," its scheduled expiration date.[20] Dunn, in a letter to White, referred to this interview and stated that he was very much surprised at this

---

[20]Dunn letter to White. 14 June 1931. 839.51/3426.

attitude because it had never before been brought into the discussions. He said that all loan negotiations had assumed that the Convention would automatically be prolonged. He added that it was very doubtful if any kind of financing could be obtained unless guaranteed under the Convention of 1924. It was his conviction, he concluded, that unless some kind of financing was arranged soon, default on the external debt was inevitable.[21]

This was the proper note upon which to terminate the discussions, for default of a limited kind had become the State Department's answer to the Dominican financial problem. As early as November 11, 1930, some seven months before these empty exercises relating to a new loan, Stimson, Cotton, White and Miller had agreed that the best alternative open to the State Department was a suspension of payments to the sinking fund of the 1922 and 1926 loans. Ruminating over this, Stimson confided to his diary that it ". . . brings up some very serious questions of our own responsibilities . . . the bonds having been made while we were in control of the government in Santo Domingo."[22] The responsibilities referred to were not only to the bondholders under the terms of the Convention of 1924 but also to the General Receiver of

---

[21]*Ibid*.

[22]Stimson. *Diaries*. X. Nov. 11, 1930. pp. 146-147.

Dominican customs. Apart from this question of legalities, the better part of political wisdom indicated that the responsibility for a moratorium must fall squarely on Trujillo's shoulders. When Cotton proposed that the State Department ask for a suspension of sinking fund payments, Stimson rejected it. Trujillo, he rightly complained, had repeatedly announced that every dollar would be paid. "Of course, that is nonsense, but it would be used against us in case of any future criticism." The position of the department would be more justifiable he argued if Trujillo was put in a situation where he had to admit "his inability to pay and put himself in a position of a bankrupt government . . . ."[23]

Suspension of amortization payments was early decided upon, then, as the solution to Dominican financial difficulties. The declaration of a suspension was to come from Trujillo and at no time would the United States officially sanction it. It did acquiesce in the measure and it would strongly intimate that such acquiescence would be forthcoming long before the step was actually taken.

For his part, Trujillo did not take the step sooner because he was anxious to protect his already dubious credit rating in the United States. Once a moratorium was declared all doors to a loan would be closed. The first intimation

---

[23] _Ibid_. Nov. 12, 1930. pp. 216-217.

that a moratorium might be acceptable came on September 6, 1930. The Bureau of Insular Affairs of the War Department had received word that the customs for that month would be insufficient to meet the obligations of the sinking fund and the Acting General Receiver had advised the arrangement of a moratorium.[24] William E. Pulliam, the General Receiver, was ordered to return to his post immediately and to make no disbursements except those incident to the expense of collections until he received further instructions.[25]

When Curtis received word of this step he pleaded with the Department to rescind the order. He argued that the situation did not warrant such action because,

> It is practically certain that customs receipts will suffice to cover the amount of interest and amortization due . . . and it (suspension of payments) would be . . . harmful to Dominican credit . . . .[26]

Curtis received his reply that same day, September 16, although it was not all that he had hoped for. He was informed that Pulliam had been instructed to remit to the fiscal agent the amount necessary to meet the interest for September. The amortization payment might also be made if that were the desire of the Dominican government. The Department, Curtis

---

[24]Secretary of War Hurley to Stimson. 6 Sept. 1930. 839.51/3256.

[25]Cotton to Curtis. 12 Sept. 1930. 839.51/3263a.

[26]Curtis to Stimson. 16 Sept. 1930. 839.51/3267.

was told, ". . . (was) suggesting that the General Receiver should take such action with respect to the sinking fund as the Dominican Government may request him to take."[27]

Thus, at this early date the State Department had approved the principle of a moratorium. The financial situation improved somewhat after September, however, at least as far as Dominican imports were concerned, and time was permitted for reconsideration of the question. Sometime during the second week of October the matter had been considered at a conference attended by Secretary Stimson, Cotton, White and Wadsworth. Apparently no memo of that conference exists but the general conclusion reached is revealed in a memo drawn up by Cotton on October 17. Referring to that conference Cotton intimated that what had been decided was to allow affairs in the Dominican Republic to drift until the efforts to negotiate new loans had run their course.[28]

Upon reflection, and after reading the Convention of 1924, Cotton wrote that he believed a "wrong conclusion" had been reached at the conference. The Convention, he stated, had been a "reckless promise" and, he continued,

> How this Department ever saw fit to risk any such convention I do not understand, but it did accept full responsibility and I do not think it can be shaken off now . . . . The Convention may have been very unwise, but we must accept it as a fact.[29]

---

[27]Stimson to Curtis. 16 Sept. 1930. 839.51/3269.

[28]Cotton memo to Stimson and White. 17 Oct. 1930. 839.51/3284.

[29]*Ibid*.

By the Convention, he wrote, the Department had assumed the role of agent or attorney for the bondholders. He believed that a moratorium should be declared at the instance of the Department of State and soon, for if this were not done the receivership would collapse and the bondholders would lose everything. A suspension of payments, he admitted, was ". . . high-handed, but it is just what a Receiver would do for a private insolvent under similar circumstances."[30]

Cotton saw two major obstacles to this solution. One, he wrote, was that the Dominicans were laboring ". . . under a fundamental misconception that they still have (had) a borrowing capacity," and it was owing to this mistaken notion that they had sent the Economic Mission to New York. Cotton predicted that the failure of this effort would not be long in coming. Secondly, the bondholders, too, were captive to a misconception. They believed, Cotton stated, that their bonds were worth more than their real value because of the arrangement of the receivership. They depended upon the State Department to see that the service of the bonds was continued. Cotton observed that he did not think ". . . anything but default will cure them." The Dominican Republic, he added, was insolvent and running a deficit of $2,000,000 a year. If something were not done to prevent it there was certain to be a financial and

---

[30]Ibid.

political crash. He concluded,

> It has been hoped hitherto that the State Department could avoid the obloquy of being the one to give the coup de grâce to the sinking fund. I do not see how. I think the State Department must be the one who commands that the sinking fund not be paid to the Fiscal Agent.[31]

The memo is a revelation in many respects. For present purposes, however, it has significance for two reasons. First, in Cotton's reference to the conference between himself, Stimson, White and Wadsworth, it is made clear that the Department had receded from its earlier position on a moratorium. At the same time, it had been decided to allow Dominican affairs to drift, to let the Dominicans bide their time in fruitless negotiations for a new loan. It is clear from Cotton's reference to the conference that no one expected success from these efforts. Certainly that was Cotton's opinion for he contended that the Republic had no borrowing capacity. Secondly, it is made clear that the Department had determined to "avoid the obloquy" of declaring a moratorium. The whole purpose of Cotton's memo had been to register his disagreement with this policy and to explain why the United States should assume a positive role in effecting a moratorium.

That he failed to change the policy decided upon is evident from the fact that only infrequent and incidental reference to a moratorium is made from November, 1930 through

---

[31]<u>Ibid</u>.

May, 1931. This was the period of active negotiation for new loans which it had been decided to let run their course.

The subject of a moratorium was renewed by the State Department immediately after negotiations for the loan with Lee, Higginson had been broken off on June 30. On July 1, Dunn visited the Department and in an interview with Herbert Feis expressed the view that little hope remained that the Dominican government could float any kind of loan. He reiterated what he had said to White on June 14, that responsibility for this situation rested with the Department because of its position regarding the extension of the life of the receivership. Feis replied that this could not be helped. The receivership, he pointed out, ". . . had been under extremely severe and steady criticism . . . ," and a continuation of it affected not only Dominican policy, ". . . but entered into our whole relationship with Latin America . . . ." It would have been inconsistent with the general Latin American policy, he told Dunn, to accept willingly a prolongation of the controls implicit in the receivership.[32] This remark casts even greater doubt on the sincerity of the proposal for the financial adviser made on February 12.

---

[32]Feis memo to Harvey H. Bundy, Undersecretary of State. 1 July 1931. 839.51/3445.

Feis had, however, a more significant statement to make to Dunn on this occasion. He said that it was recognized that some solution had to be found for the Dominican financial difficulty. If it were not, he told Dunn, default on the bond payments would result, in which event the United States would have to take steps to protect the General Receiver. He concluded,

> I imagine that if affairs approach this position (default), a way out might be found through a Dominican declaration of suspension merely of the amortization payments--in which case we might decide simply to let the situation run along.[33]

In these remarks the whole of the Department's policy toward a moratorium was revealed. In the first place, Trujillo was given an open invitation to declare a suspension of payments. At the same time, however, he would have to accept the opprobrium of the bondholders. The State Department could remain aloof from the matter excusing its inaction on the ground that nothing could be done about it. Secondly, the invitation to declare a moratorium was limited to payments on the principal of the debt. Interest payments on both bond issues were, by implication, to continue. This involved a difficult legal problem. The bond issue of 1922 held a prior lien on all customs receipts, that is, both interest and sinking fund charges on these bonds had to be paid before either the interest or principal of the 1926 bonds. The General Receiver, Pulliam, could be held personally liable for any breach of this

---

[33] Ibid.

contract. If the interest on the 1926 bonds were to be paid before the principal on those of 1922, the General Receiver could be held responsible by the holders of the 1922 bonds. Therein lay the need for his protection.

Dunn was not told how this difficulty could be surmounted. Indeed, the State Department was only dimly aware of the various complications that would arise before the matter was finally settled. It would have to take a larger hand in shaping a satisfactory moratorium than it had originally intended and it became very difficult at times to maintain an official attitude of disapproval of the measure while guiding Trujillo along the most convenient course.

The State Department had to be careful not to give the impression that it was actively promoting a moratorium in order not to arouse the criticism of bankers and bondholders. Shyness in stating its position to these interests is apparent in a memo of a conversation between Harvey H. Bundy, Assistant Secretary of State, and Jerome D. Greene of Lee, Higginson. Bundy had suggested that Lee, Higginson, as fiscal agent for the bonds, offer some relief to the Dominicans on the heavy amortization payments. He told Greene that the Department feared that if such relief was not forthcoming, the situation would become so chaotic in the Republic that repudiation of the loan would result as a product of "utter lawlessness and confusion."[34]

---

[34]Bundy memo of conversation with Greene. 11 Aug. 1931. 839.51/3459.

Greene was non-commital as to this but reminded Bundy that the United States government had an obligation to the bondholders, under the Convention of 1924, to intervene in their behalf. He asked Bundy what the attitude of the Department would be in the event of a suspension of payments. Bundy's reply was also non-commital. He said that he ". . . could not express any views on this question . . .," even though the policy of the Department had been well established. He did concede, however, that ". . . this Government was not enthusiastic about the idea of intervention in the Dominican Republic."[35]

That the State Department was conscious of the opposition of bankers to a moratorium is evident in another Department memo, unsigned, that had been passed around for general information. It was noted that the bankers were unwilling to accept a moratorium on payments to the sinking fund even though this was the only constructive measure that seemed to offer some prospect of relief to the Dominican government.[36]

The Department of State not only had to avoid, to the extent possible, offending the banking interests by appearing to remain aloof from the project, but it had, at the same time to become more intimately involved in order to prevent

---

[35]*Ibid.*

[36]Unsigned State Department memo. 29 Aug. 1931. 839.51/3473.

Trujillo from taking a rash and ill considered course. Bundy's remark to Greene regarding the need to alleviate the situation before it deteriorated into "utter lawlessness" is indicative of some apprehension in this regard. On July 27, Curtis reported that a front page article had appeared in La Opinion, a Trujillo organ, recommending suspension of payments on the debt, including the interest. Trujillo denied to Dunn that he had inspired this editorial. Curtis remarked, however, that he was "somewhat unreliably informed" that Trujillo had told others of his intention to have something of this same nature published.[37]

On August 7, Major Thomas E. Watson of the United States Marine Corps, a Trujillo crony, came to the Department and told Bundy that he, Dunn, and Trujillo had "separately" concluded that "some drastic step" should be taken in connection with a suspension of payments. Bundy replied that it would be preferable if the problem were "approached constructively by conference: between the two governments. He added that the Department was only ". . . waiting until the Dominican Republic presented its proposals as to a solution of the problem, which we would be glad to consider.[38]

On this occasion Trujillo did not hesitate long in taking up the Department's invitation. Five days later, on August 12,

---

[37]Curtis to Stimson. 27 July 1931. 839.51/3449.

[38]Bundy memo of conversation with Watson. 7 Aug. 1931. 839.51/3456.

M. L. Stafford, chargé of the American Legation in Santo Domingo, reported that Trujillo had prepared a letter to President Hoover announcing his intention to declare what in effect was a suspension of payments on the bonds issued in 1922 and 1926.[39] Trujillo's plan was sent to President Hoover on August 25, 1931. It was not an outright declaration of a moratorium. His scheme involved the issuance of $25,000,000 in new bonds to be exchanged for those issued in 1922 and 1926. The outstanding bonds totaled only $17,000,000, leaving a surplus of $8,000,000 to be used for retirement of the floating debt and a public works program. The new bonds would bear a six per cent interest rate and would be amortized at the rate of one per cent per year.[40]

On the face of it, this seemed a simple and forthright proposal for relieving the Dominican Republic of its burdensome debt payments and, at the same time, protecting the interests of the bondholders. Its simplicity, however, did not obscure the fact that it was utterly chimerical. In the first place, there were no buyers for Dominican bonds in the amount needed to carry out any of the purposes of the plan presented. Secondly, the holders of the bonds of 1922 and 1926 were not going to exchange securities the redemption

---

[39]Stafford to Stimson. 12 Aug. 1931. 839.51/3472.

[40]_For. Rel._ II. 1931. Letter from Trujillo to Hoover. 25 Aug. 1931. 839.51/3477. p. 113.

of which were due as early as September 1, 1931, and not later than 1942 for those not redeemable for nearly fifty years not to mention the dubious security of the new bonds. Furthermore, the new bonds were to be issued under the receivership, automatically prolonging its life. The United States had repeatedly stated that this was unacceptable.

Trujillo's scheme had one curious feature that was totally unacceptable to the United States. His letter to Hoover was accompanied by a copy of the proposed Dominican law providing for the implementation of his plan. Article nine of the law authorized Trujillo to suspend, at any time after October 1, 1931, payments for the service--interest as well as amortization--of any of the bonds issued in 1922 or 1926. Only the new bonds, for which the old could be exchanged, were required to be serviced.[41] This was patently an attempt to force the bondholders to exchange their existing securities for the new ones.

The immediate reaction of the State Department was firm but cautious. It had long recognized the need for some kind of moratorium but it hoped that it could be limited. Stafford was informed by telegram on September 3, that the Department saw "insuperable objections" to the plan as presented. He was instructed to state to Trujillo that it was the Department's conviction ". . . that immediate passage of the law would

---

[41]Ibid. p. 116.

prejudice constructive solution of the problem . . . ."[42] Arturo Despradel, the new Dominican Minister to Washington, was requested to urge upon Trujillo the view that his plan would render even more difficult a solution to the Dominican financial problem. The plan envisaged by Trujillo, Despradel was told, would be interpreted as a repudiation by the Dominican government of its debt and would be quite impossible to implement because of opposition by bankers and bondholders alike.[43]

The Department of State was correct in its estimate of the attitude to be taken by the bankers, who in turn represented the bondholders. A Mr. Durant of Lee, Higginson informed Bundy on September 2, that the sale or exchange of bonds for $25,000,000 was out of the question. He suggested that bonds for only the amount of the interest and amortization payments for 1931 be issued as a means of protecting the bondholders. Bundy pointed out that the United States had a responsibility to the Dominican Republic and that a measure of the type suggested by Durant would be unduly onerous to that country and would not, in any case, be in the interest of the bondholders in the long run. Durant, dissatisfied, reminded Bundy that the United States had an obligation to

---

[42]Stimson to Stafford. 3 Sept. 1931. 839.51/3477.

[43]Bundy memo of conversation with Despradel. 3 Sept. 1931. 839.51/3481.

the bondholders as well as to the Dominican Republic and urged that any plan adopted take that fact into account.[44] One week later, on September 10, W. McCormick Blair, also of Lee, Higginson, told Bundy the same thing, that the proposed bond exchange was out of the question.[45]

Trujillo, nevertheless, made one last effort to get the reconversion plan accepted. On October 8, he wrote to Lee, Higginson informing them, as fiscal agent, that the Dominican Republic could no longer meet the full service of the outstanding bonds. He suggested that the bondholders form a committee to study the proposed bond exchange or that they agree to a modification of the terms of the existing contract.[46] Blair informed Bundy that this proposal had been rejected. Nothing, he said, could be accomplished by forming a bondholders' committee because the bondholders would insist that the contract be honored as it stood.[47]

Trujillo once again gave signs of sweeping aside all obstructions and taking some unwanted independent action. On

---

[44]Bundy memo of conversation with Durant. 2 Sept. 1931. 839.51/3482.

[45]Bundy memo of conversation with Blair. 10 Sept. 1931. 839.51/3496.

[46]H. F. Arthur Schoenfeld, American Minister to the Dominican Republic, to Stimson. 8 Oct. 1931. 839.51/3522.

[47]Bundy memo of telephone conversation with Blair. 14 Oct. 1931. 839.51/3539.

September 4, Stafford reported that the Dominican Congress had passed the law empowering Trujillo to carry out all of the objects of his proposal to President Hoover. Trujillo had not signed the law but had sent it back to the legislature to be amended in such a manner that he would be authorized to suspend or reduce the amortization payments without reference to a bond exchange plan. The amended law retained, however, the authorization to issue $25,000,000 in bonds for reconversion of the debt.[48]

Dunn was in Washington a few days later and Bundy questioned him on this matter. Dunn expressed surprise that Trujillo had moved so rapidly in having the law passed authorizing the declaration of a moratorium as well as the bond issue. Before leaving Santo Domingo he had urged that nothing drastic be done until he had had the opportunity to discuss matters with the bankers and the Department of State. Bundy then told Dunn that he could not emphasize too strongly the obligations that the Department had to the bondholders. He impressed upon Dunn that United States' relations with the Dominican Republic were somewhat different from those with other Caribbean countries in that they were governed by treaty. Bundy then expressed the hope that Trujillo would do nothing requiring counter-measures by the United States that would increase its difficulties in the rest of Latin America.[49]

---

[48] Stafford to Stimson. 4 Sept. 1931. 839.51/3479.

[49] Bundy memo of conversation with Dunn. 9 Sept. 1931. 839.51/3490.

Taken together, these remarks contained the implied threat that if Trujillo persisted in his independent course the United States would have to take measures to protect the General Receiver, a right conferred upon it by the Convention of 1924. Mild in form though this implied threat was, it is significant that it was made at all. Even if it is conceded that the threat was pure bluff and that there was no intention to pursue to conclusion its serious implications, the fact that it was made is indicative once again of the reservations with which the Hoover administration approached the policy of non-intervention. Intervention was clung to as an undesirable and last resort measure to be unsheathed when necessary to protect economic interests.

Apart from this, Bundy's remarks to Dunn are further indications that the Department, in spite of any disclaimers to the contrary that it had made and would make again, was deeply involved in working out the details of a declaration of a moratorium. It was not the principle of a moratorium to which it objected but rather the form in which Trujillo had presented it. This is clear from Bundy's remarks to Despradel concerning the law submitted to the Dominican Legislature. Bundy, on September 4, told Despradel that he hoped that no action would be taken on the law until after a Department meeting concerning Dominican finances, scheduled for September 10, had been held. He said that he regarded Trujillo's recent action as most unfortunate. Despradel inquired as to what objection there was to the Dominican legislation then pending. Bundy replied that the provision of the law principally objected to was that authorizing the issue of new bonds to be exchanged for the old. This was an implied threat to the bondholders and embarrassed efforts to find a solution to the Dominican financial problem.[50]

Trujillo agreed to delay any action on the pending legislation until further efforts were made to work out some more agreeable measure.[51] Dunn had been working on this very matter and it was the reason for his trip to the United States. He had worked out the draft of a law that would allow Trujillo to suspend payments on the principal of the debt while at the same time continuing to pay the interest on both the bond issues of 1922 and 1926. When Dunn revealed this plan to Bundy, the latter replied that he did not see how the interest could be paid on bonds of 1926 before the amortization on those of 1922. Dunn argued, however, that it would do little good to suspend payment only on the amortization of the bonds issued in 1926. This amounted to less than $1,000,000 and was insufficient to meet the needs of the Dominican government.[52]

---

[50]Thurston memo of conversation between Bundy and Despradel. 4 Sept. 1931. 839.51/3495.

[51]*Ibid*. (Despradel relayed this information to Bundy.)

[52]Bundy memo of conversation with Dunn. 10 Sept. 1931. 839.51/3498.

This was, nevertheless, the plan that Dunn took with him to Santo Domingo. He left a draft of this proposal with Judge Otto Schoenrich in New York and the latter forwarded it to Bundy. The plan was not specific as to every detail but it did provide for the full service of the bonds issued in 1922 and the interest on those of 1926.[53]

Upon his return to Santo Domingo, however, Dunn reassumed his previous position. He wrote to Bundy that both he and Pulliam regarded anything short of total suspension of amortization payments as an insufficient measure. Trujillo, Dunn revealed, was willing to accept a moratorium on only the payments to the sinking fund of the bonds issued in 1926. This was acceptable to him only because it offered a precedent upon which to base future increases in the amounts to be withheld from the General Receiver.[54]

A week later Pulliam came to Washington to confer with Bundy and he confirmed Dunn's view. Nothing could be accomplished, he told Bundy, by suspension of the amortization payments on the 1926 bonds only. Bundy replied that a moratorium on the amortization of the 1922 bonds was opposed if it meant that the interest payments on the bonds of 1926 would not be paid. He added, however, that the Department

---

[53]Letter from Schoenrich to Bundy. 14 Sept. 1931. 839.51/3492.

[54]Letter from Dunn to Bundy. 26 Sept. 1931. 839.51/3516.

was waiting for word from the newly appointed Minister to the Dominican Republic, H. F. Arthur Scheonfeld, and would be guided largely by his advice.[55]

Schoenfeld arrived in Santo Domingo on October 1, and after surveying the situation, reported that he, too, saw the need to suspend all amortization payments. He stated that the serious step of declaring a moratorium was hardly worthwhile if it did not include the sinking fund payments on both bond issues. He was opposed, however, to suspending payments on the interest of the 1926 bonds and urged the Department to sell Lee, Higginson on the idea of cooperating so that this interest charge could be met before the amortization on the 1922 bonds.[56] This had already been attempted, however, and Lee, Higginson had declined to commit itself to any course that would make it liable to action by the bondholders.[57]

The impasse was finally broken by Trujillo and Dunn on October 17. The former called upon Schoenfeld that day and informed him of a plan that would suspend the payments on all amortization and at the same time continue paying interest on both bond issues. The Dominican government would simply

---

[55]Bundy memo of conversation with Pulliam. 6 Oct. 1931. 839.51/3535.

[56]Schoenfeld to Stimson. 14 Oct. 1931. 839.51/3530.

[57]Bundy memo of conversation with Blair. 10 Sept. 1931. 839.51/3496.

divert a portion of the customs receipts before they reached the hands of Pulliam, the General Receiver, relieving him of his personal liability to the bondholders. Schoenfeld wrote that in his view this plan "merited real sympathy," though, of course, it could not receive the official approval of the United States.[58]

While official approval could not be given to any kind of moratorium, the Department of State saw in this latest proposal a way out of the difficulty. It had throughout opposed the suspension of interest payments on the bonds issued in 1926. At the same time, however, it had recognized the need for a moratorium on the amortization payments of the 1922 bonds. Owing to the prior lien on Dominican customs of the latter, the General Receiver was required to meet the full service on these bonds before paying the interest on those issued in 1926. Whatever other obligation the State Department might be willing to forego meeting, it could not allow the General Receiver to bear the responsibility for violation of the contracts. For his part, Pulliam had no choice but to remit the proceeds that he collected according to the terms of those contracts. If, however, Pulliam never received the proceeds derived from customs, he could not be held responsible for their disbursement.

This was the heart of the Dominican proposal presented to the Department of State on October 20, 1931. It was

---

[58]Schoenfeld to Stimson. 17 Oct. 1931. 839.51/3541.

presented in a note that included the text of the Dominican law enabling Trujillo to take the contemplated action. The enabling act stipulated that the General Receiver would be limited to collecting only those customs sufficient to pay the expenses of the receivership and the interest on the bonds issued in 1922. All other revenues derived from customs were designated as an emergency fund to be collected under the supervision of a Special Agent for the Emergency Fund.[59] It was understood that William E. Dunn would be appointed to this post in his capacity as a financial expert hired by the Dominican government.

The enabling act stipulated the priority of accounts to be paid by the Special Agent. First to be paid from the emergency fund was the interest on the bonds issued in 1926. Second were the expenses of the Special Agent incidental to the collection of customs. Thirdly, the Dominican government was to receive $125,000 per month for use in its operations. Fourthly, any surplus in the emergency fund after these expenses had been met was to be remitted for the amortization of the bonds of 1922 and 1926. The law was to continue in force until October 31, 1933, unless economic conditions improved before that date rendering the law unnecessary.[60]

---

[59] For. Rel. II. 1931. Despradel to Stimson. 20 Oct. 1931. 839.51/3582. p. 128.

[60] Ibid. pp. 128-129.

Secretary Stimson's reply to the Dominican note was not an open approval of the step taken. He acknowledged the strenuous efforts by the Dominican government to meet all of its international obligations and expressed sympathy for it in its troublous economic condition. He also noted the salient features of the emergency law and stipulated that it would make necessary the extension of the life of the receivership. He did not, however, make any statement implying approval of the measure by the United States. In concluding his reply Stimson merely stated that it was ". . . with an understanding of the special circumstances which you (Despradel) point out that the policy of this Government will be guided."[61]

All that the United States would do then was acquiesce in the action Trujillo intended to take. In explaining this policy to Lee, Higginson, Stimson wrote that, ". . . this Government is not disposed at this time to take any action other than to continue to follow with attention and care the developments in the Dominican Republic."[62]

This is not surprising in view of the attitude the Department of State had maintained throughout the events leading to the moratorium. It had refrained at every point

---

[61] Ibid. Stimson note to Despradel. 23 Oct. 1931. 839.51/3582. pp. 131-132.

[62] Ibid. Stimson letter to Lee, Higginson and Company. 10 Nov. 1931. 839.51/3632. pp. 131-132.

from becoming openly involved in arriving at the moratorium as a solution to the Dominican financial crisis. Walter Thurston had suggested as early as August 19, 1931, that the United States become an active partner in formulating a moratorium by coming to an open agreement with Trujillo concerning such a measure. He argued that if Trujillo were allowed to circumvent the obligations of the Convention of 1924 in ex-parte fashion, that is without official approval by the United States, he might later seize the customs outright and sympathy in the hemisphere would be with him.[63]

Thurston's proposal had been rejected, however, before ever being presented. Cotton, it will be recalled, had urged a similar policy in October, 1930, which had been rejected at that time. Schoenfeld also favored an agreed upon moratorium and suggested that a modus vivendi be negotiated after the Dominican declaration of a moratorium in order to regularize the conditions that it would create.[64] He was informed that the exchange of notes between the two governments concerning the moratorium would have this effect.[65]

The Department of State was also anxious that, for the record, it be made clear that it was opposed to a moratorium.

---

[63]Thurston memo to Bundy. 19 Aug. 1931. 839.51/3494.

[64]Schoenfeld to Stimson. 14 Oct. 1931. 839.51/3531.

[65]Stimson to Schoenfeld. 15 Oct. 1931. 839.51/3531.

As late as September 10, 1931, Bundy had told Dunn, ". . . that the United States Government would certainly be no party to any default because of our duty to the bondholders . . . ."[66] But duty to the bondholders could countenance a moratorium on sinking fund payments and Bundy discussed with Dunn the means by which this could be satisfactorily accomplished. He assiduously avoided suggesting a detailed plan of how it might be done leaving this to Dunn and his employer. The thrust of Bundy's remarks clearly indicated, nevertheless, that a moratorium was not only acceptable but was being recommended.[67]

The intent of all this was to absolve the Department of State of the responsibility for the declaration of a moratorium. The purpose in giving the appearance of aloofness from the discussions leading to a moratorium and the official avowals of disapproval was to lay that responsibility at the feet of Trujillo.

The moratorium as finally arranged, however, was clearly a violation of the Convention of 1924. That treaty gave to the United States the right to protect the General Receiver when he was prevented from carrying out his duties. Since the enabling act declaring the moratorium, for all practical purposes, had removed the General Receiver from his former position, the bondholders might have expected

---

[66]Bundy memo of conversation with Dunn. 10 Sept. 1931. 839.51/3498.

[67]*Ibid*.

the United States to interfere to protect him. When Stimson explained the acquiescence of the United States in the moratorium to Lee, Higginson, however, he stated that this had been necessary for ". . . the preservation of law and order upon which the ultimate payment of the external debts must depend."[68]

Bundy's summary of the policy adopted toward the moratorium also struck this theme. Writing on October 30, he stated:

> The United States has carefully avoided being a party to any default, but when conditions in the Dominican Republic reached the point that law and order and the essential elements of Government . . . could not be maintained without diverting sums from the amortization payments of external loans, the United States Government decided not to interfere forcefully . . . even though treaty rights expressly permit interference.[69]

This statement and Stimson's remark to Lee, Higginson, were probably more in the nature of a justification to the bondholders for not taking any action than an expression of the Department's fears that political chaos in the Dominican Republic was imminent. Trujillo was firmly in control of the country at this time and there were no reports of revolutionary activity. Furthermore, the Department had expressed doubts earlier concerning Trujillo's claim that

---

[68]For. Rel. II. 1931. Stimson letter to Lee, Higginson. 10 Nov. 1931. 839.51/3632. p. 135.

[69]Bundy memo summarizing Department's policy vis-a-vis moratorium. 30 Oct. 1931. 839.51/3586.

unless a moratorium was declared orderly government would break down. On two separate occasions Bundy had requested Dunn to prepare a detailed statement supporting this claim.[70] No such evidence was forthcoming.

The explanation for acquiescence in the moratorium is the plain fact that there was no other solution to the problem. It had long been recognized that the Dominican government was in need of increased revenues. The only source from which this might be obtained was the customs receipts, since loans, small or large, had been ruled out. The customs were deficient by more than $60,000 in September, 1931, of the amount necessary for the full service of the debt. Default on at least a part of the payments was going to occur, therefore, in any case. The United States was unwilling to do anything to force the Dominican government to make up the deficiency from its internal revenues for two reasons. First, this would have required intervention which, while never openly renounced and even on occasion raised as a possible alternative, the Department of State had repeatedly made clear it was reluctant to impose because of the harm it would do to its relations with Latin America.

Secondly, even had the United States been inclined to intervene, such action would not have changed anything. Dominican revenues would have continued to decline, perhaps more sharply than before. Even honest and efficient

---

[70]Bundy memo of conversation with Dunn. 9 Sept. 1931. 839.51/3490; and, 10 Sept. 1931. 839.51/3498.

administration, which it might be assumed would have been one of the results of intervention, would not have increased Dominican revenues to the extent necessary to meet the full service of the bonds. The United States, had it intervened, might have found itself in a position of having to declare a moratorium.

A further reason for acquiescing in the moratorium was that this had been regarded by the State Department as the least complicated method of resolving the Dominican financial crisis. It has been shown that a moratorium, in principle, had been accepted as early as September, 1930. After January, 1931, every step taken by the Department led inevitably toward a suspension of the debt payments. It may have been hoped to the very last that such a measure could be avoided. That there were reservations concerning the scope of the moratorium is certain. It is equally plain, however, that a moratorium of a limited kind was preferred to any other alternative.

CHAPTER VIII

APPEASEMENT AND DRIFT

During the fifteen months left to the Hoover administration after the declaration of the moratorium, the lesson was to be learned repeatedly that Trujillo kept his commitments only when forced to do so or when it was to his advantage. In this period he sought to alter the status provided for in the law establishing the moratorium and in other ways breached the treaty relationship with the United States. In one or two instances, as will be shown, the Department of State resisted. For the most part, however, its Dominican policy was markedly lethargic. This was the result, by and large, of the apparent belief of the Department of State that, short of some degree of interference, there was nothing that could be done about the dictator's violations of extant agreements and understandings. Moreover, 1932 was an election year. The Hoover administration could ill afford the campaign burden of defending a foreign intervention even had such a policy been considered desirable on other grounds. Finally, however, Dominican affairs were of slight importance compared to domestic and other foreign problems created by the world financial crisis.

The State Department was given early warning to expect trouble from Trujillo in confining himself to the limits imposed by the emergency law. On November 14, Schoenfeld reported to Bundy that the Dominicans regarded the whole emergency program as a legal fiction arranged to accommodate the Department's scruples regarding its obligations to the bondholders under the Convention. They had very little understanding of the limitations imposed by the emergency law and apparently believed that the passage of that law was sufficient to satisfy the requirements of the State Department. They did not imagine that they would be prevented from circumventing it if that became necessary or convenient.[1]

There is the barest suggestion in Schoenfeld's observation that Trujillo and his clique were unsophisticated and well-intentioned. They were neither, of course. They did indeed regard the emergency law as a legal fiction but this attitude was the outgrowth of cynicism, not lack of sophistication. Trujillo was aware that the Department of State had insisted upon a measure of this kind in order to justify its policy to the bondholders. He apparently believed that he could violate with impunity the emergency law just as he had the Convention if he advanced slowly enough. He accepted it because it met his needs and wishes of the moment. More importantly, however, it set the precedent for more far-reaching measures.

It is difficult to understand Schoenfeld's naiveté. He had earlier indicated, however, a sympathetic understanding for the Trujillo regime. Soon after arriving at his post he reported that Trujillo's administration had only a "minimum of responsibility" for the Dominican economic crisis. The major fault,

---

[1]Schoenfeld to Bundy. 14 Nov. 1931. 839.51/3607.

according to Schoenfeld, should be placed with the corruption of the provisional government preceding Trujillo's election and with international economic conditions that had prevailed since Trujillo's inauguration.[2] For the latter, of course, Trujillo cannot be held responsible. He cannot be absolved, however, of responsibility for whatever mismanagement of public funds had occurred during the preceding provisional government of Rafael Estrella. During that period Trujillo, not Estrella, had been the real executive power and Schoenfeld was indulging in wishful thinking if he believed that the dictator was blameless for the lack of integrity in the administration of financial affairs during that time.

Schoenfeld, in one of his early dispatches, also described Trujillo as modest--this about the man who was to receive the self-conferred titles of Generalissimo, Liberator of the Republic and Benefactor of the Fatherland and after whom the capital city would be named in 1936 while he was still president--and exceptionally vigorous.[3] There can be no doubt that Trujillo was vigorous and even a very capable, albeit dishonest, administrator. Schoenfeld's impression that he was modest was very likely the result of Trujillo's capacity for obsequious behavior when circumstances seemed to require it. His inclination to conduct himself in this fashion is apparent from the same dispatch in which he was characterized as modest. Schoenfeld reported that Trujillo

---

[2]Schoenfeld to Stimson. 14 Oct. 1931. 839.51/3531.

[3]Schoenfeld to Stimson. 11 Oct. 1931. 839.51/3538.

was so disposed to rely upon the American Minister and Department of State for policy guidance that he, Schoenfeld, had to advise him that the United States was limited in its power to help the Dominican Republic.[4]

In time Schoenfeld would be disabused of any notions he held concerning Trujillo's modesty. To the extent that he was taken in at the outset of his assignment, it may have resulted from the fact that he had been sent to the Dominican Republic for the expressed purpose of gaining the confidence of the dictator in order to influence his policies. It will be recalled that Curtis had been in quite the opposite position and had been kept at arms length by Dominican officials. It had long been recognized by the State Department that Trujillo was in power to stay and that American policy had to reconcile itself to that fact. At the time that a moratorium was nearing the point of declaration, Curtis had been relieved of his assignment because he preferred intervention to allowing Trujillo to circumvent any provision of the Convention.[5]

Trujillo was aware of Curtis' attitude and could not be expected to confide in him or be influenced by him. What was needed was for someone to be sent to the Republic more disposed than Curtis had been to view the moratorium sympathetically and at the same time to establish a relationship with the dictator

---

[4]*Ibid.*

[5]Bundy memo of conversation with Curtis. 20 Aug. 1931. 839.51/3469.

that might allow the exercise of a moderating influence on his policies. This was the task assigned to Schoenfeld. Apparently no memoranda exist of the conferences between Schoenfeld and other officials of the Department of State during which these matters were discussed. The conclusion arrived at above, however, is inescapable when viewed from the logic of the situation and from Schoenfeld's dispatches from Santo Domingo.

Neither Schoenfeld nor the State Department, however, had anticipated just how far Trujillo intended to stray from the confines of the emergency law. In most instances they acquiesced in the dictator's breaches of the law and his agreements with the United States.

One of the first indications that Trujillo intended to alter the arrangement provided for in the emergency law came in connection with the expenses of the receivership. The emergency law, it will be recalled, had stipulated that the General Receiver would continue to collect customs at certain minor ports in the amount necessary to pay the expenses of the receivership and the interest on the bond issue of 1922. According to Article one of the Convention of 1924, which remained in force allowing for exceptions required by the emergency law, the expenses of the receivership had priority over all other accounts to be paid by the General Receiver. The allowance for these expenses, however, was limited to five per cent of the total collections of any given month. The practice, since 1924, had been for the General Receiver to withhold the full five per cent each month and to remit the surplus to the Dominican government at the end of each fiscal year.

This practice enabled the General Reciever to make up for any month's expenses in excess of the five per cent allowance from the following month's receipts. With the exception of 1930, there had always been a surplus in the allowance at the end of the year.[6]

The emergency law provided that the Special Agent for the emergency fund would provide the General Receiver with funds sufficient to pay the expenses of the receivership and, of course, the interest on the bonds issued in 1922, if his own collections fell short. The emergency plan had been designed to make certain that the collections supervised by the General Receiver would fall short of his needs. This was deemed less of a danger than allowing him to collect more than he needed, since any balance that he might have over and above the amount necessary for these expenses had to be remitted for amortization of the bond issue of 1922. Now, however, that the General Receiver was dependent upon Trujillo for the sums needed to pay the expenses of the receivership, the Dominican dictator was not disposed to provide him with the full five per cent allowance each month. On December 4, 1931, Trujillo proposed that only an amount sufficient for each month's expenses, plus the interest installment, rather than the whole five per cent allowance be remitted to the General Receiver by the Special Agent. Pulliam informed Schoenfeld of his fear that the Dominican government might not provide

---

[6]Pulliam to Secretary of War Hurley. 16 June 1930. 839.51/3225.

for the deficit in any month that the five per cent allowance was insufficient. Moreover, this procedure would establish a precedent which Trujillo might use after the expiration of the emergency law.[7]

Schoenfeld, when reporting this to the Department, wrote that he had received assurances from Trujillo and Dunn that in any month that expenses of the receivership should exceed five per cent they would see that the deficiency was provided for out of the emergency fund. Schoenfeld disregarded Pulliam's fear that a bad precedent might be established and advised against making any representations at that time on the grounds that the whole procedure of the emergency law was admittedly irregular and it would serve no useful purpose to raise an issue over a technicality in its operation.[8] In its reply the Department informed Schoenfeld that it concurred fully in his view.[9]

This particular matter was closed at that point and Schoenfeld reported in January of 1932 that the transfer of funds from the Special Agent to the General Receiver had gone smoothly.[10] There was no reason why it should not have since the amount was only a small portion of the total derived from customs. Trujillo knew how to keep a bargain when all of the advantages accrued to him. Aside from this, however, the episode illustrates Trujillo's

---

[7]Schoenfeld to Stimson. 4 Dec. 1931. 839.51/3647.

[8]*Ibid*.

[9]Stimson to Schoenfeld. 5 Dec. 1931. 839.51/3647.

[10]Schoenfeld to Stimson. 13 Jan. 1932. 839.51/3367.

disposition to probe and test the determination of the State Department to resist his violations of agreements. He had gotten by with a revolution, a fraudulent election and a suspension of the sinking fund payments on the external debt. He was prepared to see how much further he would be permitted to go.

Schoenfeld was incorrect in predicting that protests by the United States would do no good. Trujillo was as prepared to retreat as he was to advance. This is illustrated in connection with Dominican insistence that the approval by the Dominican government of the General Receiver's budget was required. Article five of the Convention of 1924 stipulated that the accounts of the General Receiver were subject to "examination and verification" by the Dominican government as well as by the proper American authority, the Bureau of Insular Affairs of the War Department. In practice, the Dominican government had never exercised its right to inspect the books of the receivership. In the summer of 1930, however, Trujillo had ordered such an inspection, which order had been carried out during the weeks immediately preceding the declaration of a moratorium.[11]

In December, 1931, Creed F. Cox, Chief of the Bureau of Insular Affairs, visited the Republic for his own annual inspection of the receivership but also to determine what had been the Dominican purpose in doing so. Cox approached Rafael Vidal,

---

[11]Schoenfeld to Stimson. 18 Dec. 1931. 839.51/3651. (While the Dominican Customs Receivership was under direct supervision of the Bureau of Insular Affairs of the War Department, policy decisions and instructions on all substantial issues came from the Department of State.)

Trujillo's right-hand henchman and Minister of Finance at that time, concerning the matter. He told Vidal that the Bureau was prepared to give its "friendly consideration" to any recommendations that the Dominicans might wish to make as a result of the inspection.[12] Vidal told Cox that the Dominican government hoped that out of the inspection the principle could be established that its approval of the budget and the expenditures of the receivership would be required as well as that of the Bureau. Cox asked if this had been prompted by some discrepancy in the accounts of the General Receiver. It was not at all a matter of complaint, Vidal replied, but one of principle.[13]

The United States had interpreted the Convention to mean that the Dominican government could only examine accounts of the receivership and had reserved to itself the sole right of approving its budget. Pulliam was deeply concerned about the recent inspection and Vidal's explanation of it. Schoenfeld reported that Pulliam feared that it was merely the first step to the more far-reaching demand to control specific items in the budget. Schoenfeld agreed but reported that he did not feel anything could be done about it because of the provision in the Convention.[14]

Trujillo let the matter rest until March, 1932, when he requested a copy of the budget of the receivership in order that the accounts might be audited. Edwin C. Wilson of the Latin

---

[12] Ibid.

[13] Schoenfeld to Stimson. 22 Dec. 1931. 839.51/3657.

[14] Schoenfeld to Stimson. 24 Feb. 1932. 839.51/3698.

American Affairs Division told Despradel, the Dominican Minister, that a copy had been supplied with the understanding that it was for purposes of information only. Despradel replied that that may have been the case but he understood that his government would soon raise the question of its right to approve the budget. Wilson countered bluntly that it was not believed that the Convention would support the Dominican government to this extent.[15]

Thus apprised of the opposition of the Department of State Trujillo dropped the matter and never raised it again. This whole affair is of only minor importance except as it illustrates that Trujillo could be resisted without resulting in an immoderate but undefined reaction on his part. The ease with which he was discouraged on this issue suggests that, perhaps, it would have served some useful purpose to oppose him on other more significant occasions.

All the while that this issue was being discussed, Trujillo was moving on other fronts. It will be recalled that the emergency law provided for the payment of the expenses of the Special Agent and that $125,000 be supplied monthly to the Dominican government. Any surplus in the emergency fund after these amounts had been deducted was to be remitted for amortization. In January, 1932, Dunn came to Schoenfeld and stated that he shared with Trujillo the view that the surplus in the emergency fund could be held over from month to month rather than applying it to the sinking fund. This would assure the Dominican government of

---

[15]Wilson memo of conversation with Despradel. 26 Mar. 1932. 839.51/3714

realizing the full annual allotment of $1,500,000 ($125,000 per month) allotted to it by the emergency law after privileged expenses--receivership expenses and interest--had been adequately provided for. Any surplus remaining at the end of the year would then be remitted for amortization. Dunn argued that if the surplus were remitted each month, the Dominican government would have no fund to draw upon during those months when customs fell so low that they could not provide the monthly allotment of $125,000.[16]

In his account of this discussion Schoenfeld reported that he had told Dunn that he did not believe that the United States could accept this interpretation. On the other hand, he pointed out that the question need not be raised at all. He suggested that the matter of remitting the surplus to the fiscal agent for amortization was largely one of when it was most advantageous for the retirement of bonds. If the price of the bonds appeared to be declining it would be to the advantage of the Dominican government to wait until the end of the year to apply the funds to their retirement.[17] In other words, the Dominican government could hold funds over from one month to the next but could not support such action by reasons of the emergency law.

Winthrop R. Scott of the Latin American Affairs Division disagreed with Schoenfeld's rationale. In a memo to Bundy he argued that to permit the Special Agent, Dunn, to withhold the surplus of one month to provide for a possible deficiency of the next was a penalization of the bondholders. Scott felt that the

---

[16]Schoenfeld to Stimson. 7 Jan. 1932. 839.51/3664.

[17]*Ibid*.

Department had "gone rather far" to accommodate the Dominican government in the matter of its financial distress and in allowing it to bypass treaty relationships. This had been unavoidable, he wrote, but the contemplated measure of holding over monthly surpluses was a radical departure from the original intent of the emergency law. Scott saw no merit in the contention that this would allow the retirement of the bonds on terms most advantageous to the Dominican Republic. He pointed out that the fiscal agent would do this anyway once the money was in the sinking fund. He concluded with the recommendation that the Department insist on the ". . . substantial carrying out of the terms of the emergency legislation."[18]

Schoenfeld's view was upheld in this instance and no protest was registered with the Dominican government and it continued its practice of withholding the surplus. On March 4, 1932, Scott drew up a memo for general Departmental consideration listing a number of violations of the emergency law. He noted that the law had provided for a priority of accounts to be paid out of the emergency fund of $125,000. Second only to current government operating expenses was the debt owed to the Red Cross resulting from the hurricane of 1930. After the law had been in operation for three months, however, the Red Cross had not been paid, but back government salaries, last on the priority list, were being paid.[19]

Another violation of the emergency law had been the

---

[18]Scott memo to Bundy. 15 Jan. 1932. 839.51/3676.

[19]Scott memo summarizing Dominican affairs. 4 Mar. 1932. 839.51/3707.

allocation of $250,000 per year to an account under the direct control of Trujillo. There were no controls whatever on the disbursements from this fund, which had not been provided for in the emergency law in any case. Scott pointed out that the floating debt was also being increased, violating the law in spirit at least. One of the purposes of the emergency law had been to provide the Dominican government with additional revenue so that it would no longer need to issue domestic bonds. Further evidence that Trujillo was ignoring the spirit of law was the cool reception given to Dunn's plan for instituting budgetary responsibility.[20]

Scott's campaign for a stronger Dominican policy nearly succeeded. On April 9, Schoenfeld was informed that ". . . the Department feels that a firm insistence at an early stage to prevent substantial deviation from the spirit of the Emergency Plan may prevent a much more serious situation later."[21] He was instructed to bring to the attention of Trujillo the various matters referred to in Scott's memorandum. The instruction was qualified to the extent that Schoenfeld could make representations regarding these matters at his own discretion.[22]

That Schoenfeld intended to be excessively discreet is apparent from his reply to these instructions. He recommended that the Department not make an "isolated point" of certain of

---

[20] *Ibid.*

[21] White to Schoenfeld. 9 Apr. 1932. 839.51/3720A.

[22] *Ibid.*

the complaints listed by Scott. He recommended further that if the Department felt it necessary to say anything to the Dominican Minister, Despradel, concerning these matters that it be softened with approving remarks about the efforts that the Dominican government had been making at fiscal responsibility.[23]

This approach to dealing with Trujillo had not been effective in the past and would not be on this occasion. He merely interpreted it as a further indication that the Department of State would not obstruct him in his violation of the emergency law. That is, in fact, what it was but Schoenfeld's attitude prevailed, nevertheless.

Trujillo's boldness in violating the spirit and the letter of the emergency law is seen most clearly in his expenditures for military equipment at a time when he was purportedly initiating fiscal reform. The State Department had learned that a Major Figueroa of the Dominican army had been in the United States seeking credit in the amount of $100,000 for the purchase of military aircraft. A telegram to Schoenfeld signed by Stimson raised strong objections to this. It was stated that, "The Department desires to know . . . why Dominican Government considers it necessary to incur these expenses at a time when it cannot meet the amortization on its outstanding loans." The telegram concluded with the reminder that this was an increase in the public debt requiring approval by the United States.[24]

23Schoenfeld to Stimson. 19 Apr. 1932. 839.51/3723.

24Stimson to Schoenfeld. 4 Feb. 1932. 839.51/3677A.

Schoenfeld, in an interview with Trujillo, sought an explanation. Trujillo boldly denied that Major Figueroa had been authorized to enter into any such negotiations. He had been assigned the task of looking into the specifications of such equipment for future need. The planes would not be purchased until the money had been saved out of the regular army budget. Trujillo added that even then no purchases would be made without first consulting the Department of State.[25]

Schoenfeld than asked if it were true that $50,000 worth of army uniforms had been purchased on credit--the Department had informed him of this but said that nothing could be done because the contract had already been consummated.[26] Trujillo admitted that this was so.[27] He had done this without "consulting" the Department but Schoenfeld failed to account for the obvious discrepancy between his conduct and his announced good intentions.

Trujillo also evaded in not very subtle fashion the objections to the purchase of the airplanes. On February 19, Trujillo came to the Legation and told Schoenfeld that Figueroa had returned to report that he had found the desired military planes and that they could be purchased for $50,000. Trujillo reiterated that no order would be placed until the army budget showed a savings large enough to permit it and then only after the United States had been consulted. He informed Schoenfeld,

---

[25]Schoenfeld to Stimson. 5 Feb. 1932. 839.51/3678.

[26]Stimson to Schoenfeld. 4 Feb. 1932. 839.51/3677A.

[27]Schoenfeld to Stimson. 5 Feb. 1932. 839.51/3678.

however, that two airplanes costing $20,000 each had been purchased by the National School of Aviation for the purpose of starting a commercial service.[28]

When Schoenfeld reported this to the Department he added that he had checked the Legation files and discovered that this organization had been in existence since August 27, 1929, and that Trujillo had been elected as its president in that year.[29] Trujillo's explanation of the purchase of two airplanes and Schoenfeld's confirmation of the existence of the National Aviation School placed an innocent face on the transaction. If, however, one is not inclined to be suspicious of any explanation offered by Trujillo, there is positive proof that he was prevaricating in this instance. On March 7, 1932, the Department of State learned that the two airplanes purchased for "commercial use" had been equipped to carry two thirty caliber Browning machine guns and standard bombs.[30] Again, however, the Department declined to make any protest in the face of an accomplished fact. It is not surprising that Trujillo felt safe in violating his agreements with the United States. He gained much and never seemed to lose anything even on those rare occasions when the United States resisted.

Trujillo had openly violated the provisions of the emergency law before it had been in operation two months. He had allocated

---

[28]Schoenfeld to Stimson. 17 Feb. 1932. 839.51/3689.

[29]*Ibid.*

[30]Scott memo. 7 Mar. 1930. 839.51/3708.

$7,000,000 of the emergency fund, which totaled only $1,500,000, for the retirement of a portion of the floating debt. The emergency law had made no provision for this whatsoever. Moreover, in a conference at the State Department between Scott and Bundy it had been observed that the liquidation of the floating debt with funds from customs was a direct violation of the rights of the bondholders who had a prior claim to the customs receipts. The amortization payments on their bonds had been suspended because of the supposed need of the Dominican government. If funds were not available for the payment of this debt it was difficult to see why they should be allocated for the retirement of another. It was decided, nevertheless, to raise no objection to this measure on the ground that in the long run the retirement of the floating debt could possibly enhance the value of bonds representing the external debt.[31]

Other matters arose throughout the remaining months of the Hoover administration, the funding of the floating debt, that is, making it permanent in theory as well as in practice; the modification of the emergency law to divert more of the customs receipts to the Dominican government; and numerous instances of financial mismanagement wasting the advantages that were supposed to have accrued from the emergency law. These violations of the emergency law and agreements with the United States were either tolerated or carried over into the New Deal period. In either case they serve as further evidence of the passive character of

---

[31]Scott memo of conference with Bundy, 7 Dec. 1931, 839.51/3673.

the Dominican policy of the Hoover administration during its last months in office.

The purpose in relating the response by the United States to these several violations by Trujillo of his commitments has not been to berate American policy makers for failing to take the measure of the dictator. It is evident, however, that any policy attempting to exert a moderating influence upon Trujillo was doomed to failure unless accompanied by a determination to insist that he comply with previous agreements. No tyrant will keep an inconvenient commitment when he is aware that painful consequences will not result from its breach.

The reasoning that it served no purpose to protest these violations does not stand up under close examination. It has been shown that on the one occasion in which the State Department mildly rebuked Trujillo--when he asserted the right to approve the budget of the Receiver General--he retreated in haste. On the occasion of the purchase of the aircraft, he was rather desperately dishonest in an attempt to cover his offense. It was, as the State Department feared, very possible that on any given occasion Trujillo may have gone ahead with his intention in spite of an official protest by the United States. This may have chilled relations for a time but the United States would have been no worse off than before. Trujillo would have been hesitant to take such a step in any case. He had much to lose by alienating the United States because his only hope for a lasting solution to Dominican financial difficulties was through cooperation with his northern neighbor.

There is, however, a more significant point to be made concerning this aspect of the Dominican policy of the Hoover administration. Appeasing Trujillo was unlikely to bring the desired result of improving the hemispheric relations of the United States. The conduct of its relations with the Dominican dictator did not offer any opportunity to charge the United States with intervention, it is true. But for a nation to be considered a "good neighbor," more is required than mere immunity from criticism. It requires that its policies have the respect and confidence of other nations. Dominican policy in this period commanded neither.

CHAPTER IX

CONCLUSIONS

From the foregoing review of Hoover's Dominican policy several conclusions can be drawn regarding his approach to Latin America as a whole. It is recognized, of course, that any statement made concerning that policy, when drawn from United States-Dominican relations alone, has its limitations. An area of the size and including as many countries as Latin America cannot usually be treated as a unit. Clearly, a distinction must be made between Caribbean policy and policy for South America. From its earliest days, the United States has viewed the Caribbean as having special significance for the nation's security. By the twentieth century, security interests had become an all too available pretext for interfering in the internal affairs of the Caribbean republics. As has been shown, Hughes and Stimson were at pains to make this distinction and invoked the national security rationale to defend intervention in the Caribbean should it become necessary. What is equally clear, however, is that South Americans failed to appreciate the distinction. No thoughtful observer can seriously argue with Norman Davis' comment that intervention in a Caribbean republic was as much resented in South American states as if they had been the victim.[1]

---

[1]Davis. "Wanted: A Consistent Latin American Policy." p. 563.

During the period under study Dominican affairs presented the whole array of challenges which in the twentieth century had evoked from the United States the kind of response most resented by its hemispheric neighbors. Therefore, the way these challenges were met by the Hoover administration ought to be indicative of its Caribbean policy in general.

The most obvious conclusion to be drawn from Hoover's Dominican policy is that, after 1929, the United States was limited in its power to influence the course of events in the Republic. Beset by financial crisis at home and abroad the Hoover administration had not the reserve of energy to impose its will on the Dominican political and financial crisis. The distractions created by the international depression were in themselves sufficient to discourage the strong policy required if the United States were to dictate the solution to the Dominican revolution and "election" of 1930 or the moratorium of 1931. Moreover, intervention would not have increased Dominican revenues and, thus, its ability to pay the bondholders. Harvey Bundy dealt with this matter in a final report on Dominican affairs in 1933. On the question of the suspension of amortization payments, he wrote that

> . . . the United States decided not to intervene forcefully . . . even though treaty rights expressly permit interference. The decision is based upon the belief that interference would benefit neither nation and would not help the bondholders.[2]

---

[2]Stimson Papers. Series VI. Selected State Department Documents. Box 239, Folder #3. p. 22.

It is interesting to note that the decision not to intervene was a deliberate one. In other words, it was a decision taken because its opposite would not serve the purpose and not because it stemmed from an established policy of non-intervention. If further proof of this is needed, Bundy's concluding remarks provide it.

> A determination of a policy of non-interference in this particular case was not reached until investigation by the Department . . . confirmed the necessity of the emergency action adopted in order to preserve orderly government in the Dominican Republic.[3]

What is clear form this is that the decisions to intervene or not to intervene would be made in each case as it arose. No commitment to a policy of non-intervention was ever established as a guide to the handling of any particular case.

While the United States was in no position to influence the course of the Dominican political and financial crisis, it is clear also that the policy of non-interference was aimed at improving its relations with its hemispheric neighbors. It is clearly evident from the State Department records that the official correctness maintained during the revolution and election that brought Trujillo to power was intended to keep the United States clear of charges of interference. It has been shown repeatedly that instructions from the Department of State impressed this attitude upon its representatives in Santo Domingo.

---

[3]*Ibid*. pp. 22-23.

It cannot be maintained, however, that the Good Neighbor Policy originated with Hoover. The single most important conclusion to be drawn from this study is that Hoover's Latin American Policy was not the forerunner to the later Good Neighbor Policy. Even his apologists concede that, whatever Hoover's intentions were, his policy did not win many friends in the hemisphere for the United States. Hoover's policy failed because it was negative. It provided no leadership for Pan-Americanism, or "the Western Hemisphere idea." Nor did it present any program for inter-American action to cope with the problems arising out of the depression. On the contrary, the Smoot-Hawley Tariff, signed into law by Hoover, aggravated the economic problems in Latin America arising out of the depression.

Hoover's Latin American policy fell short of anticipating the Good Neighbor Policy for another more significant reason. The heart and soul of the Good Neighbor Policy formulated by the administration of Franklin Roosevelt was its commitment to absolute non-intervention. This commitment was made publicly at Motevideo in 1933, albeit with the qualification that the United States retained its rights as a sovereign nation under international law. At the Inter-American Conference held at Buenos Aires in 1936, this commitment was proclaimed without any reservation. It was this pledge to non-intervention which gave credibility to other aspects of the Good Neighbor

Policy. It was this commitment that broke down the barriers of distrust and suspicion and opened the door to a greatly improved relationship between the United States and its hemispheric neighbors.

The Hoover administration had never been prepared to make the commitment to absolute non-intervention. While intervention was never exercised during the years of this administration it was an instrument held in reserve with the implied threat that it might be used under given circumstances. This reservation in Hoover's policy has been shown in three specific instances in Dominican relations. It will be recalled that during the revolution Curtis had requested that naval vessels be sent to the Republic to counter potential danger to American lives and property. Cotton refused to comply with this request unless and until actual depredations had occurred. While no interference of the kind proposed by Curtis was exercised, it is clear that the United States reserved to itself the right to do so and admitted of conditions under which it might be undertaken.

This same reservation was implicit in the attitude of the State Department towards Trujillo's election. It did not intend to do anything to prevent Trujillo from gaining the presidency. It will be recalled again, however, that in a letter to Secretary of the Interior Wilbur, Cotton conceded that marines might be sent to the Republic as a "last resort." He did not state explicitly what he meant by this but it is likely that he feared destruction of American lives and property and/or interference with the operation of the receivership. If any of these potential dangers developed intervention would be considered as a "last resort." None of these events did occur, however, and no decision had to be made regarding the dispatch of marines to the Republic. It is significant, nevertheless, that, whatever Cotton may have had in mind, intervention was held in reserve as a possible alternative. And if it was regarded as an unwanted and undesirable alternative, so had been every other instance of intervention in the twentieth century.

Another example of the reservation in the attitude of the Hoover administration towards intervention has been shown in connection with Trujillo's precipitate action regarding the moratorium. The dictator, already assured of American acquiescence in the principle of a moratorium, had caused the Dominican legislature to pass a bill authorizing the declaration of a suspension of the payments on the principal of the external debt. The reaction to this measure by the Department of State was shown in Bundy's remarks to Dunn. Bundy reminded Dunn that the United States, by the terms of the Convention of 1924, had an obligation to the bondholders to protect the General Receiver in order that he might fulfill his responsibilities. Bundy then warned Dunn that Trujillo's precipitate action, if persisted in, might require the United States to respond in such a way as to increase its difficulties in the rest of Latin

America. He did not explain what form this response would take. The implication is clear, however, that he contemplated strong measures likely to incur criticism from the rest of the hemisphere.

It is doubtful that on this occasion it was seriously intended to intervene unless, perhaps, Trujillo completely ignored the advice of the State Department. Again, however, it is significant that the warning was issued at all. Had there been a commitment to non-intervention there would have been no occasion to allude to the subject.

To a large extent, it was because of the reservations held with respect to intervention that Hoover's efforts to improve United States-Latin American relations failed. Had non-intervention been Hoover's declared policy this would have been justification for crediting him with initiating the Good Neighbor Policy. As it was, however, non-intervention was not placed within the context of an avowed commitment to that policy. The reason for not having made a declaration to this effect is clear. The Hoover administration was unprepared to make any such commitment. It has been shown conclusively that on at least three occasions in its relations with the Dominican Republic intervention, or the threat of it, was proposed as an alternative policy to be used in the event that a specific situation developed.

Bibliography

Sources

Herbert Hoover Papers. Files: Cabinet Officers; Correspondence; Diplomats; Foreign Affairs. Herbert Hoover Library. West Branch, Iowa.

Henry L. Stimson Papers. Files: Speeches, Writings, Statements; Selected Documents of the State Department. Manuscripts and Archives, Yale University Library. New Haven, Conn.

Henry Stimson Diaries. X-XV. Manuscripts and Archives, Yale University Library. New Haven, Conn.

The National Archives of the United States. Diplomatic, Legal and Fiscal Branch. The files primarily used in the preparation of this study were: 839.51, the financial relations between the United States and the Dominican Republic; and, 839.00, the reports of the internal conditions in the Dominican Republic. Other files researched were: 711.39, the political relations between the United States and the Dominican Republic; 839.00 Revolutions, the Dominican revolution of 1930; 839.00 Trujillo, Rafael L., documents pertaining to the personal and public record of the Dominican president; 839.00 Presidential Visits, pertaining to the visit of Horacio Vasquez to the United States in 1924; 839.00 Presidential Campaigns, concerning aspects of the Dominican election of 1930; 839.51 Wadsworth Mission, relating to the visit by Eliot Wadsworth to investigate the economic conditions of the Dominican Republic in 1930; 839.51 Economic Mission, reports on the activities of the Dominican Economic Mission seeking a loan in the United States in 1930. Two other fiels researched were: 033.3911 and 611.3931, both in reference to the discussions held at Washington during the Vasquez visit in 1924 concerning the most favored nation agreement and the revision of the Convention of 1907.

Published Documents

Stimson, Henry L. "The United States and the other American Republics." United States Department of State. Publications. No. 156. Latin American Series, No. 4.

United States Department of State. Memorandum on the Monroe Doctrine. (Prepared by J. Reuben Clark). Washington, D. C., 1930.

United States Department of State. Papers Relating to the Foreign Relations of the United States. Vol. 1, 1922; Vol. 1, 1923, Vol. 1, 1924; Vol. 2, 1925; Vol. 2, 1927; Vol. 2, 1930; Vol. 2, 1931; Vol. 5, 1932; Vol. 4, 1933. Washington, D.C.

Books

Besault, Lawrence De. President Trujillo: His Work and the Dominican Republic. (Second Edition). Washington, D. C., 1936.

Blakeslee, George H. The Recent Foreign Policy of the United States. New York, 1925.

Calcott, Wilfrid Hardy. The Caribbean Policy of the United States, 1890-1920. Baltimore, 1942.

Current, Richard N. Secretary Stimson: A Study in Statecraft. New Brunswick, N. J., 1954

DeConde, Alexander. Hoover's Latin American Policy. Stanford and London, 1951.

Dozer, Donald. Are We Good Neighbors? Three Decades of Inter-American Relations, 1930-1960. Gainesville, Florida, 1959.

Espaillat, Arturo R. Trujillo: The Last Caesar. Chicago, 1963.

Ferrell, Robert H. American Diplomacy in the Great Depression: Hoover Stimson Foreign Policy, 1929-1933. New Haven, Conn.,

Galindez, Jesus De. La Era De Trujillo. Santiago de Chile, 1956.

Gardner, Lloyd C. Economic Aspects of New Deal Diplomacy. Madison, Wisc., 1964.

Gonzalez-Blanco, Pedro. La Era de Trujillo. Ciudad Trujillo, Dominican Republic, 1955.

Guerrant, Edward O. Roosevelt's Good Neighbor Policy. Albuquerque, New Mexico, 1950.

Haring, Clarence H. South America Looks at the United States. New York, 1928.

Hicks, Albert C. Blood in the Streets: The Life and Rule of Trujillo. New York, 1946.

Hoover, Herbert. Memoirs II. New York, 1952.

Hughes, Charles Evans. Pan American Peace Plans. New Haven, Conn., 1929.

Hughes, Charles E. Our Relations to the Nations of the Western Hemisphere. Princeton, 1928.

Jimenes-Grullon, J. I. Una Gestapo en America. La Habana de Cuba, 1946.

Jimenez, R. Emilio. Biografia de Trujillo, Ciudad Trujillo, Dominican Republic, 1955.

Knight, Melvin M. The Americans in Santo Domingo. New York, 1928.

Link, Arthur S. Wilson. Vol. 2. The New Freedom. Princeton, New Jersey, 1956.

________. Wilson. Vol. 3. The Struggle for Neutrality. Princeton, New Jersey, 1960.

Mecham, J. Lloyd. A Survey of United States - Latin American Relations. Boston and New York, 1965.

Munro, Dana Gardner. Intervention and Dollar Diplomacy in the Caribbean, 1900-1921. Princeton, New Jersey, 1964.

Myers, William Starr (Compiler and editor). The State Papers and Other Public Writings of Herbert Hoover. Vol. 1. New York, 1934.

________. The Foreign Policies of Herbert Hoover, 1929-1933. New York, 1940.

Nanita, Abelardo R. Trujillo. (Fifth Edition). Ciudad Trujillo, Dominican Republic, 1954.

Nevins, Allan. Hamilton Fish: The Inner History of the Grant Administration. 2 vols. (Revised Edition). New York, 1957.

Ornes, German E. Trujillo: Little Caesar of the Caribbean. New York, 1958.

Perkins, Dexter. Hands Off. A History of the Monroe Doctrine. Boston, 1941.

________. The United States and the Caribbean. Cambridge, Massachusetts, 1947.

Sanchez Lustrino, Gilberto. Trujillo: Constructor du une Nacionalidad. Habana de Cuba, 1938.

Schoenrich, Otto. Santo Domingo, a Country with a Future. New York, 1918.

Tansill, Charles Callan. The United States and Santo Domingo, 1798-1873: A Chapter in Caribbean Diplomacy. Baltimore, 1938.

Vega y Pagan, Ernesto, Lieutenant, Dominican Navy. Military Biography of Generalissimo Rafael Leonidas Trujillo Molina. (Translated by Ida Espaillat). Ciudad Trujillo, Dominican Republic, 1956.

Walker, Stanley. Journey toward the Sunlight. New York, 1947.

Welles, Sumner. Naboth's Vineyard. The Dominican Republic, 1844-1924. 2 vols. New York, 1928.

________. The Time for Decision. New York and London, 1944.

Whitaker, Arthur P. The Western Hemisphere Idea: Its Rise and Decline. Ithaca, New York, 1954.

Wood, Bryce. The Making of the Good Neighbor Policy. New York, 1961.

Articles

Baughman, C. C., Commander, United States Navy. "United States Occupation of the Dominican Republic." United States Naval Institute, Proceedings. Vol. 51 (1925), 2306-2327.

Bernard, L. L. "What Our Latin American Neighbors Think of Us." The Historical Outlook. Vol. 19 (1923), 363-367.

Buell, Raymond. "Changes in Our Latin American Policy." Annals. American Academy of Political and Social Sciences. Vol 156 (1931), 126-132.

________. "A New Latin American Policy." Forum. Vol. 81 (1928), 113-118.

________. "The Intervention Policy of the United States." Annals. American Academy of Political and Social Sciences.

Cambon, Jules. "La Doctrine de Monroe en 1928." Rev. des Deux Monde. Vol. 47 (1928), 90-101.

Chapman, Charles E. "The United States and the Dominican Republic." Hisp. Am. Hist. Rev. Vol. 7 (1927), 84-91.

Cleven, N. A. N. "Mr. Hoover Concludes Goodwill Mission in South America." Current History. Vol. 29 (1929), 852-855.

Corwin, Edward S. "The Monroe Doctrine." North American Review. Vol. 218 (1923), 721-735.

Davis, Norman. "Wanted: A Consistent Latin American Policy." Foreign Affairs. Vo.. 9 (1931), 547-568.

DeConde, Alexander. "Herbert Hoover's Good Will Tour." Historian. Vol. 12 (1950), 167-181.

Hardy, Osgood. "Rafael L. Trujillo." Pacific Historical Review. Vol. 15 (1946), 409-416.

Hollander, Jacob H. "The Convention of 1907 between the United States and the Dominican Republic." Am. Jour. of International Law. Vol. 1 (1907), 287-296.

Hughes, Charles Evans. "Centenary of the Monroe Doctrine." International Conciliation. No. 154 (1924).

Hughes, Charles E. "The Monroe Doctrine after 100 Years." Current History. Vol. 19 (1923), 102-113.

________. "Observations on the Monroe Doctrine." American Journal of International Law. Vol. 17 (1923), 601-623.

Kelsey, C. "The American Intervention in the Dominican Republic and Haiti." Annals. Am. Acad. of Pol. and Soc. Sci. Vol. 100 (1922), 109-199.

Knapp, H. S., Rear-Admiral, United States Navy. "The Naval Officer in Diplomacy." Proceedings. United States Naval Institute, Vol. 53 (1927), 309-317.

Rippy, J. Fred. "Initiation of the Customs Receivership." Hisp. Am. Hist. Rev. Vol. 17 (1937), 419-457.

Rochester, H. A., Lieutenant, United States Navy. "The Navy's Support of Foreign Policy." Proceedings. United States Naval Institute, Vol. 47 (1933), 1491-1500.

Sheppard, William R. "The Monroe Doctrine Reconsidered." Pol. Sci. Quar. Vol. 39 (1924), 35-66.

Stimson, Henry L. "Bases of American Foreign Policy." Foreign Affairs. Vol. 11 (1933), 383-396.

Vreeland, Michael. "Gunmen of Diplomacy." Am. Mercury. Vol. 6 (1925), 215-222.

Welles, Sumner. "Memorandum on Inter-American Affairs, 1933." (Ed. by Charles C. Griffin). Hisp. Am. Hist. Rev. Vol. 34 (1954), 190-192.

Whitaker, Arthur Preston. "From Dollar Diplomacy to the Good Neighbor." Inter-Am. Econ. Affairs. Vol. 4 (1951), 12-19.

Williams, William A. "Latin America: Laboratory of American Foreign Policy in the 1920's." Inter-American Economic Affairs. Vol. 9 (Autumn, 1957) 3-30.

Appendices

APPENDIX I

The Convention of 1907

Convention Between the United States and the Dominican Republic Providing for the Assistance of the United States in the Collection and Application of the Customs Revenues of the Dominican Republic

Whereas, a convention between the United States of America and the Dominican Republic providing for the assistance of the United States in the collection and application of the customs revenues of the Dominican Republic, was concluded and signed by their respective Plenipotentiaries at the City of Santo Domingo, on the eighth day of February, one thousand nine hundred and seven, the original of which convention, being in the English and Spanish language, is word for word as follows:

Whereas during disturbed political conditions in the Dominican Republic debts and claims have been created, some by revolutionary governments, many of doubtful validity in whole or in part, and amounting in all to over $30,000,000 nominal or face value:

And Whereas the same conditions have prevented the peaceable and continuous collection and application of National revenues for payment of interest or principal of such debts or for liquidation and settlement of such claims; and the said debts and claims continually increase by accretion of interest and are a grievous burden upon the people of the Dominican Republic and a barrier to their improvement and prosperity;

And Whereas the Dominican Government has now effected a conditional adjustment and settlement of said debts and claims under which all its foreign creditors have agreed to accept about $12,407,000 for debts and claims amounting to about $21,184,000 of nominal or face value, and the holders of internal debts or claims of about $2,028,258 nominal or face value have agreed to accept about $645,827 therefor, and the remaining holders of internal debts or claims on the same basis as the assents already given will receive about $2,400,000 therefor, which sum the Dominican Government has fixed and determined as the amount which it will pay to such remaining internal debts holders; making the total payments under such adjustment and settlement, including interest as adjusted and claims not yet liquidated, amount to not more than about $17,000,000.

And Whereas a part of such a plan of settlement is the issue and sale of bonds of the Dominican Republic to the amount of $20,000,000 bearing five per cent interest payable in fifty years and redeemable after ten years at 102½ and requiring payment of at least one per cent per annum for amortization, the proceeds of said bonds, together with such funds as are now deposited for the benefit of creditors from customs revenues of the Dominican Republic heretofore received, after payment of the expenses of such adjustment, to be applied first to the payment of said debts and claims as adjusted and second out of the balance remaining to the retirement and extinction of certain concessions and harbor monopolies which are a burden and hindrance to the commerce of the country and third the entire balance still remaining to the construction of certain railroads and bridges and other public improvements necessary to the industrial development of the country;

And Whereas the whole of said plan is conditioned and dependent upon the assistance of the United States in the collection of customs revenues of the Dominican Republic and the application thereof so far as necessary to the interest upon and the amortization and redemption of said bonds, and the Dominican Republic has requested the United States to give and the United States is willing to give such assistance:

The Dominican Government represented by its Minister of State for Foreign Relations, Emiliano Tejera, and its Minister of State for Finance and Commerce, Federico Velasquez H., and the United States Government, represented by Thomas C. Dawson, Minister Resident and Consul General of the United States to the Dominican Republic have agreed:

ARTICLE I

That the President of the United States shall appoint a General Receiver of Dominican Customs, who, with such Assistant Receivers and other employees of the Receivership as shall be appointed by the President of the United States in his discretion, shall collect all the customs duties accruing at the several customs houses of the Dominican Republic until the payment or retirement of any and all bonds issued by the Dominican Government in accordance with the plan and under the limitations as to terms and amounts hereinbefore recited; and said General Receiver shall apply the sums so collected, as follows:

First, to paying the expenses of the receivership; second, to the payment of interest upon said bonds; third, to the payment of the annual sums provided for amortization of said bonds including interest upon all bonds held in sinking fund; fourth, to the purchase and cancellation or the retirement and cancellation pursuant to the terms therof of any of said bonds as may be directed by the Dominican Government; fifth, the remainder to be paid to the Dominican Government.

The method of distributing the current collections of revenue in order to accomplish the application thereof as hereinbefore provided shall be as follows:

The expenses of the receivership shall be paid by the Receiver as they arise. The allowances to the General Receiver and his assistants for the expenses of collecting the revenues shall not exceed five per cent unless by agreement between the two governments.

On the first day of each calendar month the sum of $100,000 shall be paid over by the Receiver to the Fiscal Agent of the loan, and the remaining collection of the last preceding month shall be paid over to the Dominican Government, or applied to the sinking fund for the purchase or redemption of bonds, as the Dominican Government shall direct.

Provided, that in case the customs revenues collected by the General Receiver shall in any year exceed the sum of $3,000,000, one half of the surplus above such sum of #3,000,000 shall be applied to the sinking fund for the redemption of bonds.

ARTICLE II

The Dominican Government will provide by law for the payment of all customs duties to the General Receiver and his assistants, and will give to them all needful aid and assistance and full protection to the extent of its powers. The Government of the United States will give to the General Receiver and his assistants such protection as it may find to be requisite for the performance of their duties.

ARTICLE III

Until the Dominican Republic has paid the whole amount of the bonds of the debt its public debt shall not be increased except by previous agreement between the Dominican Government and the United States. A like agreement shall be necessary to modify the import duties, it being an indispensable condition for the modification of such duties that the Dominican Executive demonstrate and that the President of the United States recognize that, on the basis of exportations and importations to the like amount and the like character during the two years preceding that in which it is desired to make such modification, the total net customs receipts would at such altered rates of duties have been for each of such two years in excess of the sum of $2,000,000 United States gold.

ARTICLE IV

The accounts of the General Receiver shall be rendered monthly to the Contaduria General of the Dominican Republic and to the State Department of the United States and shall be subject to examination and verification by the appropriate officers of the Dominican and the United States Governments.

ARTICLE V

This agreement shall take effect after its approval by the Senate of the United States and the Congress of the Dominican Republic.

Done in four originals, two being in the English language, and two in the Spanish, and the represenatives of the high contracting parties signing them in the City of Santo Domingo this 8th day of February, in the Year of our Lord 1907.

Thomas C. Dawson
Emiliano Tejera
Frederico Velasquez H.

APPENDIX II

The Convention of 1924

Convention Between the United States and the Dominican Republic, Signed on December 27, 1924, to Replace the Convention of February 8, 1907.

Whereas a convention between the United States of America and the Dominican Republic providing for the assistance of the United States in the collection and application of the customs revenues of the Dominican Republic, was concluded and signed by their respective Plenipotentiaries at the City of Santo Domingo, on the eighth day of February, one thousand nine hundred and seven; and

Whereas that convention was entered into to enable the Dominican Government to carry out a plan of settlement for the adjustment of debts and claims against the Government; and

Whereas, in accordance with that plan of settlement, the Dominican Republic issued in 1908, bonds to the amount of $20,000,000, bearing 5 per cent interest, payable in 50 years and redeemable after 10 years at 102½, and requiring payment of at least 1 per cent per annum for amortization; and

Whereas additional obligations have been incurred by the Dominican Government in the form of the issuance, in 1918, of bonds to the amount of $5,000,000, bearing 5 per cent interest, payable in 20 years, and redeemable at par on each interest date as the amount of amortization fund available on such interest dates will permit, and requiring payment of at least 5 per cent per annum for amortization; and in the form of the issuance of bonds, in 1922, to the amount of $10,000,000, bearing 5½ per cent interest, payable in 20 years, and redeemable after 8 years at 101. and requiring payment after such period of at least $563,916.67 per annum for amortization; and

Whereas certain of the terms of the contracts under which these bonds have been issued have proven by experience unduly onerous to the Dominican Republic and have compelled it to devote a larger portion of the customs revenues to provide the interest and sinking fund charges pledged to the service of such bonds than is deemed advisable or necessary; and

Whereas it is the desire of the Dominican Government and appears to be to the best interest of the Dominican Republic to issue bonds to a total amount of $25,000,000, in order to provide for the refunding on terms more advantageous to the Republic of its obligations represented by the bonds of the three issues above mentioned still outstanding and for a balance remaining after such operation is concluded to be devoted to permanent public improvements and to other projects designed to further the economic and industrial development of the country; and

Whereas the whole of this plan is conditioned and dependent upon the assistance of the United States in the collection of customs revenues of the Dominican Republic and the application thereof so far as necessary to the interest upon and the amortization and redemption of said bonds, and the Dominican Republic has requested the United States is willing to give such assistance:

The United States of America, represented by Charles Evans Hughes, Secretary of State of the United States of America; and the Dominican Republic, represented by Senor Jose del Carmen Ariza, Envoy Extraordinary and Minister Plenipotentiary of the Dominican Republic in Washington, have agreed:

ARTICLE I

That the President of the United States shall appoint, a General Receiver of Dominican Customs, who, with such Assistant Receivers and other employees of the Receivership as shall be appointed by the President of the United States in his discretion, shall collect all the customes duties accruing at the several customs houses of the Dominican Republic until the payment or retirement of any and all bonds issued by the Dominican Government in accordance with the plan and under the limitations as to terms and amounts hereinbefore recited; and said General Receiver shall apply the sums so collected, as follows:

First, to paying the expenses of the receivership; second, to the payment of interest upon all bonds outstanding; third, to the payment of the annual sums provided for amortization of said bonds including interest upon all bonds held in sinking fund; fourth, to the purchase and cancellation or the retirement and cancellation pursuant to the terms thereof of any of said bonds as may be directed by the Dominican Government; fifth, the remainder to be paid to the Dominican Government.

The method of distributing the current collections of revenue in order to accomplish the application thereof as hereinbefore provided shall be as follows:

The expenses of the receivership shall be paid by the Receiver as they arise. The allowances to the General Receiver and his assistants for the expenses of collecting the revenues shall not exceed five per cent unless by agreement between the two Governments.

On the first day of each calendar month shall be paid over by the Receiver to the Fiscal Agent of the loan a sum equal to one twelfth of the annual interest of all the bonds issued and of the annual sums provided for amortization of said bonds and the remaining collection of the last preceding month shall be paid over the Dominican Government, or applied to the sinking fund for the purchase or redemption of bonds or for other purposes as the Dominican Government shall direct.

Provided, that in case the customs revenues collected by the General Receiver shall in any year exceed the sum of $4,000,000, 10 per cent of the surplus above such sum of $4,000,000 shall be applied to the sinking fund for the redemption of bonds.

ARTICLE II

The Dominican Government will provide by law for the payment of all customs duties to the General Receiver and his assistants, and will give to them all needful aid and assistance and full protection to the extent of its powers. The Government of the United States will give to the General Receiver and his assistants such protection as it may find to be requisite for the performance of their duties.

ARTICLE III

Until the Dominican Republic has paid the whole amount of the bonds of the debt, its public debt shall not be increased except by previous agreement between the Dominican Government and the United States.

ARTICLE IV

The Dominican Government agrees that the import duties will at no time be modified to such an extent that, on the basis of exportations and importations to the like amount and the like character during the two years preceding that in which it is desired to make such modification, the total net customs receipts would not at such altered rates have amounted for each of such two years to at least 1½ times the amount necessary to provide for the interest and sinking fund charges upon its public debt.

ARTICLE V

The accounts of the General Receiver shall be rendered monthly to the Ministry of Finance and Commerce of the Dominican Republic and to the State Department of the United States and shall be subject to examination and verification by the appropriate officers of the Dominican and the United States Governments.

ARTICLE VI

The determination of any controversy which may arise between the Contracting Parties in the carrying out of the provisions of this Convention shall, should the two Governments be unable to come to an agreement through diplomatic channels, be by arbitration. In the carrying out of this agreement in each individual case, the Contracting Parties, once the necessity of arbitration is determined, shall conclude a special agreement defining clearly the scope of the dispute, the scope of the powers of the arbitrators, and the periods to be fixed for the formation of the arbitral tribunal and the several stages of the procedure. The special agreement providing for arbitration shall, in all cases, be signed within a period of three months from the date upon which either one of the Contracting Parties shall notify the other Contracting Party of its desire to resort to arbitration. It is understood that on the part of the United States, such special agreements will be made by the President of the United States by and with the advice and consent of the Senate thereto, and on the part of the Dominican Republic, shall be subject to the procedure required by the Constitution and laws thereof.

ARTICLE VII

This agreement shall take effect after its approval by the Contracting Parties in accordance with their respective Constitutional methods. Upon the exchange of ratifications of this convention, which shall take place at Washington as soon as possible, the Convention between the United States of America and the Dominican Republic providing for the assistance of the United States in the collection and application of the customs revenues, concluded and signed at the City of Santo Domingo on the 8th day of February, 1907, shall be deemed to be abrogated.

Done in duplicate in the English and Spanish languages at the City of Washington this 27th day of December, nineteen hundred and twenty-four.

Charles Evans Hughes
J.C. Ariza

APPENDIX III

Dominican Emergency Law Declaring a Moratorium on Payment of the Foreign Debt

Emergency Law Referring to the Services of the Cominican Debt
Approved October 31, 1931

The National Congress
in the Name of the Republic

An Emergency Having Been Declared

Whereas the national revenues have diminished to such an extent and the needs of the Treasury are so pressing that the provision of immediate relief, pending the refunding of the national debt, is unavoidable;

Whereas a state of economic emergency exists in the Republic and in the entire world, which requires extraordinary provisional measures to provide for the needs of the moment;

Whereas it is necessary for the relief of the Treasury to suspend the payment of the excessive service of the sinking funds of our foreign 5½ per cent bonds and devote the amounts so released to the satisfaction of the most urgent items of the budget;

Whereas the Republic orders such suspension under the exigencies of a special situation and with the firm intention to resume compliance with all its obligations as soon as circumstances permit;

By virtue of the powers conferred by Article 33 of the Constitution of the State, has passed the following law:

Number:

Article 1. There is designated as an emergency fund the total amount of customs duties paid during each month in the customs houses of the Republic after the General Receivership of the said custom houses has covered in the order which is indicated: a) The expenses of the General Receivership of customs; b) The monthly installment of interest on the foreign bonds of the Republic, loan of 1922.

Article 2. The financial expert now in the service of the Government shall act as Special Agent and shall administer the said emergency fund. The amounts constituting said fund shall be received and paid out by him in accordance with the provisions of the law.

Article 3. The General Receivership of Customs shall continue to collect in each month the amounts designated in Article 1 of this law under letters (a) and (b). When the said amounts have been collected by the Receivership, all the other amounts payable as customs revenues shall be paid directly to the Special Agent of the emergency fund.

Article 4. The executive power shall issue the regulations necessary to carry out the purposes of this law.

Article 5. The compensation of 5 per cent guaranteed by the Convention of 1924 (Article 1) on total customs revenues shall suffer no diminution whatsoever on account of the present law.

Article 6. No payment shall be made from the emergency fund except by the Special Agent or a Delegate of his. From the said emergency fund the following payments shall be made in the order indicated below:

a) Payment of the monthly installment of interest on the foreign bonds of the Republic of the loan of 1926, which shall be paid to the Fiscal Agent of the said loan:

b) Expenses authorized by the executive power to cover harbor services and other expenses hitherto paid by the General Receivership of Customs for the Dominican Government; expenses of the office of the Special Agent of the emergency fund;

c) Payment to the Dominican Government of a monthly amount not to exceed One hundred twenty-five thousand pesos American gold ($125,000.00), which shall be applied to the following objects in the order indicated:

(1) Payment of the monthly deficiency, if any, in the 70 per cent of the monthly revenues of the general funds of the Nation destined for the payment of salaries.

(2) Payment of the debt of the Dominican National Red Cross, occasioned by the hurricane of September, 1930, up to the maximum sum of Two hundred Thousand dollars American gold ($200,000), and in accordance with the official list of that organization.

(3) Payment of current expenses in the same order as that specified in Law No. ....., dated ....., in case of deficiency in the general funds of the Nation.

(4) Any balance, if such there be, of the said maximum amount of One hundred twenty-five thousand dollars American gold ($125,000) shall be applied to the payment in equal amounts of salaries in arrears and expenses in arrears.

d) Any excess in the custom house revenues after payment of the amounts stated assigned to the purposes mentioned in this Article shall be paid over by the Special Agent of the emergency fund to the Receiver General of Customs to be applied to the payment of the monthly installments of amortization on the foreign bonds of the Republic.

Article 7. Whenever the total general fund revenues of the Nation during any six months' period of the fiscal year 1932 or 1933 shall amount to the sum of Two Million Two Hundred Fifty Thousand dollars American gold ($2,250,000), the present emergency law shall be without effect.

Article 8. During the life of this law none of the general fund revenues of the Nation now in existence shall be specialized, nor shall the laws which have created them be modified or repealed if such modification or repeal reduces or abolishes any of the said revenues.

Article 9. This law shall become effective on the day of its publication and shall continue in force until the end of the year 1933 unless the circumstances which have prompted the passage of this emergency law change, in accordance with Article 7.

Article 10. This law repeals all laws or provisions of laws that may be contrary thereto.

INDEX